*epitaph for a peach*

# epitaph for a peach

*four seasons on my family farm*

## DAVID MAS MASUMOTO

HarperOne
*An Imprint of* HarperCollins*Publishers*

HarperOne

An earlier version of the prologue appeared in the
*Los Angeles Times,* August 16, 1987.

EPITAPH FOR A PEACH: *Four Seasons on My Family Farm.*
Copyright © 1995 by David Mas Masumoto.

HarperCollins Web Site: http://www.harpercollins.com

HarperCollins®, ♛®, and HarperOne™ are trademarks of
HarperCollins Publishers.

Illustrations by Paul Buxman

FIRST HARPERCOLLINS PAPERBACK EDITION PUBLISHED IN 1996

Masumoto, David Mas
Epitaph for a peach : four seasons on my family farm /
David Mas Masumoto.
ISBN 978-0-06-251025-9
1. Masumoto, David Mas.  2. Peach growers—California—
Biography.  3. Japanese American farmers—California—
Biography.  4. Farm life—California.  5. Peaches—
California.  I. Title.
S417.M366A3   1995
634'.2584'092—dc20
[B]   94-39527

20 21  LSC (H)  40 39 38 37 36 35 34

*For Mom and Dad*
*and Marcy, Nikiko, and Korio*

# contents

# epitaph for a peach

The last of my Sun Crest peaches will be dug up. A bulldozer will be summoned to crawl into my fields, rip each tree from the earth, and toss it aside. The sounds of cracking limbs and splitting trunks will echo throughout the countryside. My orchard will topple easily, gobbled up by the power of the diesel engine and the fact that no one seems to want a peach variety with a wonderful taste.

Yes, wonderful. Sun Crest tastes like a peach is supposed to. As with many of the older varieties, the flesh is so juicy that it oozes down your chin. The nectar explodes in your mouth and the fragrance enchants your nose, a natural perfume that can never be captured.

Sun Crest is one of the last remaining truly juicy peaches. When you wash that treasure under a stream of cooling water, your fingertips instinctively search for the gushy side of the fruit. Your mouth waters in anticipation. You lean over the sink to make sure you don't drip on yourself. Then you sink your teeth into the flesh, and the juice trickles down your cheeks and dangles on your chin. This is a real bite, a primal act, a magical sensory celebration announcing that summer has arrived.

The experience of eating a Sun Crest peach automatically triggers a smile and a rush of summer memories. Eating a Sun Crest reminds us of the simple savory pleasures of life.

My dad planted our Sun Crest orchard twenty years ago, and those trees paid my college tuition. But now they are old and obsolete. Stricter and stricter quality standards coupled with declining demand cut deeply into production levels. Our original fifteen acres and 1,500 trees have been reduced to a patch of 350.

I'm told these peaches have a problem. When ripe, they turn an amber gold rather than the lipstick red that seduces the public. Every year the fruit brokers advise me to get rid of those old Sun Crests. "Better peaches have come along," they assure me. "Peaches that are fuller in color and can last for weeks in storage."

I have a recurring nightmare of cold-storage rooms lined with peaches that stay rock hard, the new science of fruit cryonics keeping peaches in suspended animation. There is no room there for my Sun Crests, all of them rejected with the phrase NO SHELF LIFE stamped in red across each box.

"Consumers love the new varieties," brokers advise. "They'll abandon your old Sun Crests."

My sales returns at the end of each growing season confirm their comments. Demand remains weak and I have to accept lower prices. But I can't give up. I often picture shoppers picking a Sun Crest out of one of my boxes, not knowing the hidden treasure that awaits them. When they bite into it they'll say, "Aah. *This* is a peach!"

I've been keeping those old peaches for years, rationalizing that it's worth hanging on to something that has meaning beyond mere monetary reward. But I'm scared. Scared because I can't sell my peaches; thousands of boxes sit in storage, blacklisted with a bad reputation. Boxes that have been paid for, fruit that cost me and my family, a year's labor wasted, unproductive and impotent.

Many family farmers with fruit varieties like Sun Crest peaches no longer calculate how much they earn but how much they owe. Can you imagine working an entire year and having your boss inform you that you owe him money? No matter what you believe, you can't farm for very long and only be rewarded with good-tasting peaches.

This year will witness not only the possible death of this peach but also the continuing slow extinction of the family farmer. A fruit variety is no longer valued and a way of life is in peril. My work remains unrewarded.

When I first started, I realized I would never make a fortune in farming, but I hoped I could be rich in other ways—and maybe, just maybe, my work would create some other kind of wealth in the process.

Part of me knows I'll survive. The family farmer is a tough species, and we will find ways to continue. But when I think of that Sun Crest orchard, it hurts to see a slice of my life ripped out, flavor lost along with meaning. Life will be different without Sun Crest peaches, and with the loss of variety consumers will be the ultimate losers.

I envision my orchard yielding to the bulldozer and the trees tumbling without a fight. I imagine setting a match to them and listening to the crackle of dry leaves as the dead branches are engulfed by rising flames. I estimate the embers will last for days, glowing in the chill of the fall nights.

I'll plan on going out daily to watch the fire, my face and arms warmed by the heat of the burning wood. Later I'll plow the ashes back into the earth. The ground will be renewed, and I'll hope that my next orchard will become as rich. Are my Sun Crest peaches obsolete? This, it seems, is my epitaph for a peach.

*epitaph for a peach*

Frustrated and desperate, I wrote about my peaches and sent the story to the Los Angeles Times. It was published and syndicated across the nation. In the following weeks I received dozens of phone calls and letters, strangers urging me to "keep the last good-tasting peach." These were city folk who care about the foods they eat and sympathized with my plight. For them, food has meaning beyond mere nourishment. They longed to be connected to farming.

The day the bulldozer arrived, I met it out in the fields and stopped it from entering my Sun Crest orchard. I decided to keep those trees for one more harvest.

This year carries special burdens. Working harder will not necessarily be the salvation for my peaches nor will discovering a new market for a single season. Every year my orchards and vineyards require more and more inputs of fertilizer, pesticides, and labor. I'm forced to try and increase production and find myself eyeing my neighbor's farm with thoughts of expanding and wondering, *How long can he survive?* But increased inputs do not always result in increased productivity; nature doesn't seem to work linearly. Larger farms are not necessarily more efficient; in good years huge operations may perform better, but in bad years they risk large-scale disaster.

I have been trying to farm a new way, working with, and not against, nature, which always requires a certain risk and willingness to experiment. This year will decide my fate. I can't afford to dabble in trial and error. This year I commit myself to saving those peaches; if I fail, I will have to admit my failure as a farmer. I break the spring earth with a new resolve to redeem not only one block of peaches but also my chosen life.

# chapter one

# spring work

## *Breaking Winter's Crust*

The challenge begins in early spring with the first work of the year. Disks break the hardened topsoil. The cold winter gives way to the warmth of longer days, life stirs in dormant trees and grapevines. A first irrigation feeds the delicate pale-green shoots of new growth, and legions of weeds awaken from hibernation.

Every year my muscles ache from that first workday of spring. I end by planting myself on the steps of our farmhouse porch. I lean against the rails, kick off my boots, and feel the heat rise from my sore feet. My shirt sticks to my back from the first good sweat of the year. Closing my eyes, I recall a story about work, like the hard work of this first day of spring.

A Nisei, or second-generation Japanese American, recalls his childhood lesson. His father was an immigrant who had carved out a life in America through hard work. The family lived the immigrant's success story, arriving in a new land with nothing but dreams, making opportunities for themselves by working in the fields, and eventually getting a place of their own. Everything was accomplished through one method—the ethic of hard work.

The Nisei explains: "You know how those immigrants were about work. Japanese only happy and healthy if they're working." He pauses, lets out a soft sigh, and grins. "My folks worried so much about me growing up the right way, I swear they planted weeds to make sure I always had enough work to keep me busy."

Every year, my spring work begins with that story.


## Planting Seeds

In the early spring, the earth lies bare and naked, with not much growing between the grapevines and trees. Cover crops—clovers, vetches, beans, and barley—can be planted to add nourishment and a green color of life to the fields.

I grew up playing hide-and-seek and other games, with my brother and sister in the lush fields of the cover crops. The family dog, Dusty, would come trotting after me, panting and smiling. I'd shoo her away, begging her not to disclose my location, but she'd stand next to me, wagging her tail. It didn't take long to be discovered. (Later I realized old Dusty followed me because I was the only kid she could keep up with.) Still, it was a glorious few minutes of hiding, the grasses cool to the side of my face. I could watch a ladybug crawling up my arm and feel the goose bumps spreading over my body as I tried not to flinch. I remember looking up at the pale blue sky and listening to a gentle breeze rustling through the tall grass. Often the wind would be an innocent whisper, at other times it could howl. Enveloped by nature, a child's imagination soars. The cover crops brought another world to our fields of play.

One season my dad stopped growing cover crops because of the extra work of planting seeds, irrigating, and battling weeds. Like many farmers, my dad believed that cover crops were just a cheaper source of plant nutrients until he could afford synthetic fertilizers. He explained that work was easier when plant nutrients came in bags, with guaranteed nitrogen contents. And with synthetic fertilizers, the kids could help spread the granules. I remember sitting on the back of a vineyard wagon with Dad while my brother drove the tractor (he drove because I couldn't reach the clutch pedal). Dad and I would clench old coffee cans and scoop out the fertilizer with them, tossing half a can at the base of each peach tree. My old work gloves felt like oversized baseball mitts, and my little fingers could barely bend the leather into a curl around the can. After a few hours, though, I could hold it more easily; something in the fertilizer caused the leather to stiffen, and the gloves became frozen in a death grip around the metal can.

I hope to renew the practice of cover cropping. I am part of a generation of grape and tree fruit farmers who never planted clover or beans or barley. I plant a vine and expect it to last a lifetime; a peach tree should last decades. Annual crops feel odd and peculiar—I don't know how to prepare beds and am not used to planting something underground that would be out of sight for weeks. Many of my generation never learned how to sow seeds.

I planted my very first cover crop eight years ago when my first child was born. I didn't do it because cover crops would be good for the soil and build up organic matter. And I didn't do it to provide a habitat for beneficial insects to overwinter and make my land their spring home.

I did it because my wife would be home with a new baby and she was tired of seeing only the gray earth of winter outside our kitchen window. I did it for her dreams of spring walks through the soft clover with the baby in her arms, breathing in the fresh scent of spring growth. I did it for reasons that seemed disconnected with farming at the time.

I planted my cover crops in autumn, motivated by a vision of lush fields by spring. I didn't have a seeder, so at first I tried using an old fertilizer spreader to broadcast the seeds. It sort of worked, but the seeds poured from the outlets at the beginning of a row while near the end the flow was reduced to a trickle. Instead of a nice blend, most of the smaller seeds fell first, leaving the larger ones behind, with some of the largest seeds, like the fava beans, sliced in half by the spreader gears.

Caught up in a pioneer spirit, I then tried sowing a row by hand until my arm ached from carrying the bucketfuls of seed (I was planting at only twenty pounds an acre but I had eighty acres to plant). I ended up on a tractor, throwing seeds over my shoulder with one hand while steering with the other. "Let them fall where they may," I said to myself.

Our daughter was born in early November. By Thanksgiving we had a smiling, cooing child and a germinating cover crop, its green leaves poking through the soil crust. Both child and crop grew through the winter and by spring we took walks through the fields, picking fresh peas and beans and letting ladybugs tickle her soft baby skin.

Later an organic farmer friend introduced me to the real benefits of cover crops, how they improve soils and work as a habitat for insects. "You start with the soil and build from there," he explained. He called it "growing your way back to natural farming."

Cover crops have a multiplier effect. Their lush growth adds organic matter to the earth. Earthworms return to my farm because of the healthy jungle of roots to crawl within. Moisture from the winter rains is held by a dense underground mat of clover roots. Insects breed, prolific in their wild and rank homes.

Planting these cover-crop seeds is my first step to save my Sun Crests. I begin by planting hope—hope that the seeds will germinate, hope that they will add life to the farm and even help save the wonderful taste of my fruits.

I had no training to be a father, I could only hope I'd learn quickly, on the job. As I grew my first cover crop, I had a similar feeling. I hoped an enriching harvest would follow. Babies and planting seeds: they demand that you believe in the magic and mystery of life.

Planting cover crops is more art than work. Subtle differences in each field will affect my seed selections. Some areas of my eighty-acre farm have sandy soils, others have more clay, one area is a low land, another we call "the hill" stands four feet higher than its neighbors. They all add to a diversity and create a patchwork, arranged into small five- or six-acre blocks of vines or peaches.

I like growing a variety of cover crops. The vines on "the hill" are designated for crimson clover, my young peach trees need a healthy start of vetch, the wine grapes enjoy a solid stand of strawberry clover and New Zealand white clover. I feel like Georges Seurat and his "dot, dot, dots," each seed becoming a dot on my farm canvas.

Selecting seeds is simple; planting them continues to be a challenge each year. Hand sowing from a tractor works well for a few acres but grows tedious for eighty acres. Looking for an alternative, I located an old set of Planet Jr. Seeders, a modern implementation of a simple old tool—a hopper with seeds and a roller wheel. With each turn of the wheel, a gear opens a hole and a seed drops from the hopper. The Planet Jr. Company improved the idea, adding gears and a few more moving parts while trying to keep the basic concept simple. The machine works well in smooth, clean fields like the one a vegetable grower may have prior to planting. But vines and orchards are filled with bits of trash—twigs, stems, and sticks—which take time to decompose and love to lodge themselves in Planet Jr. gears.

I discovered this one year in the spring, six months after I had seeded a field. I noticed gaping bare spots in the rows, places where little was growing. At first I thought some disease had ravaged the cover crops, then I imagined birds stealing my precious seeds. But upon closer examination, just where the bald spot ended, I found a tuft of clover or vetch, as if the seeds were piled upon one another. I concluded that the seeds must have jammed in the planter, then poured out all at once when freed.

I've thought of buying a better planter, something adapted to vineyards instead of vegetable beds. But I've become attached to my Planet Jrs. They remind me of a simple age, and I like the name. I also enjoy controlling each individual planter. Unlike an eight-foot-wide, single-hopper machine that uniformly plants an entire field with the same seed mix and in the same pattern, these individual units can be adjusted to create different patterns with a variety of seed combinations. I play artist in my fields, painting with a blend of clover and vetches with a splash of wildflowers. Next to a vine I can plant dense cahaba white vetch that would dominate in the early spring canvas with its white blooms but may begin to wither with the first heat of summer. Along another edge I might weave in some crimson clover with its deep red seed heads or scatter strawberry and red clovers for variety. I would add a combination bur clover and a blanket of yellow flowers with the green hues created by different medics, low-growing but sturdy plants that creep along the surface and replace the wilting vetches and crimson clovers in our valley heat.

My fields have become a crazy quilt of cover crops, a wild blend of patterns, some intended, some a product of nature's whims. The different plants grow to different heights and in different patterns, creating a living appliqué. The casual passerby might not notice my art. From the roadside, it often looks like irregular growth, bald spots, breaks in uniformity. But the farmer walking his fields can feel the changing landscape beneath his boots, he can sense the temperature changes with the different densities of growth and smell the pollen of blooming clover or vetch or wildflowers. He appreciates the precarious character of nature. As if running your fingers over a finely crafted quilt, you can feel pattern upon pattern. Just as a quilter may stitch together emotions with each piece of fabric, I weave the texture of life into my farm.

## Wildflowers

I plant wildflowers because they look pretty and because my wife, Marcy, likes them. Marcy believes farms should be green the year round. She was raised on a goat dairy where they grew alfalfa most of the year. She met each spring and summer day with a view of lush green growth. Now she wants our farm to be green all the time. She wants to see things growing in the fields even in winter. She longs to look out her kitchen window and see life. During the winter most of the farms in our valley lie dormant. Even in spring while the grapes push new buds, the rest of the landscape lies barren, stripped of weeds and life. Not ours.

In 1984 the market for peaches and grapes collapsed. Farms all over the San Joaquin Valley lost money, which often resulted in the birth of "the new farm wife," not a worker in the fields but a main source of income from *off* the farm.

Since Marcy and I married, the IRS has classified me as a farmer only half the time. For the other years, Marcy's off-the-farm income has been higher than mine and the farm revenue has been relegated to "other income" status. One result: in order to keep farming I had to please my banker, in this case my wife. Hence the wildflowers.

I visited other farms with lush green stands of cover crops, long slender stalks of rye or barley shimmering in the spring breeze, waves of grain growing dense and high. Farmers walk through the seas of green, plants often waist high, and hold up their arms as if fording a river. A biologist friend and I watched one farmer show us his fields and proudly speak of his new-found belief in the magic of cover crops. Later my friend whispered, "I guess it's hard to change a lifetime of farming."

I asked what he meant.

He answered, "That farmer has a fantastic stand of rye and barley. But he still thinks of simplistic monocropping. He needs to think of complexity and diversity."

My friend further explained that adding a cover crop helps soils regain organic matter. It also provides habitat for insect life. But like those of the proud farmer, my first cover crops also lacked diversity. I still grew them the same way I farmed the rest of my fields: one crop, one method, one goal. My farm lacked the chaos of diverse plant life. It was easy to see; my fields lacked blooming flowers.

Our farm changed a decade ago, with lousy prices and a realization that if the land wasn't going to make money, I might as well try to enjoy not making money. At the same time I better make life pleasing to those who are earning an income.

Once, out of desperation, Marcy bought some flowers from Kmart and stuck them on the grapevine berms. Without daily watering, they began to wilt until I began to hand water each one. For a few weeks they continued blooming and I cursed each time I had to carry a coffee can of water for them. There had to be a better way to grow flowers in the fields.

Soon afterward a friend gave me some wildflower seeds and I tossed in a handful with my cover crops. In California we've experienced periods—sometimes several years—of prolonged drought, and with the lack of consistent winter rains, my cover crops did not grow well, but the wildflowers bloomed magnificently. Marcy and I watched their sequence of bloom, the poppies first, then lupine, bachelor buttons, and daisies. She was happy, I was content, and the farm began to look better.

Now each year I scatter new seeds, the wildflowers reseed, and we watch the fields repaint themselves. The wildflowers have little to do with better prices for grapes, raisins, or peaches, but they start each year with beauty.

THE WILDFLOWERS ARE always the first plants to bloom. I sense a race for survival as they germinate and flower quickly, sprinting to procreate before the harsh, desertlike valley conditions doom a family of poppies or lupines. They also are the first to attract insects.

"Flowers open up a new world of life," said my biologist friend. "Anything blooming attracts life from miles and miles. The pollens and nectar act like huge welcome signs."

My wildflowers are early-season welcome mats for insects riding air currents, journeying into the valley from their winter homes, often in the nearby foothills. My farm sits along their tradewinds, a beckoning landfall in the barren, lifeless desert landscape. I imagine these insects to be like explorers, setting forth and sailing into the sea of vineyards and orchards. My wildflowers are sirens luring these sailors to safe and friendly islands.

After years of drought everyone has finally become concerned over the use of water. At last we're treating water as a limited resource. Nothing knows this better than the wildflowers.

Wildflowers like the California poppy continue an ancient struggle to maintain a niche in the arid ecology of the San Joaquin Valley. I've talked with allergy specialists who claim that some plants actually create extra pollen in drought years. With a lack of rain, germination, pollination, and seed production must take place within a limited window of opportunity, and I have noticed that my wildflowers seem to produce more pollens with cycles of drought.

How does this fit with my farming? I'm not sure. I water my farm artificially, so I don't think my vines or trees really feel the drought. But in the last few years, there hasn't been a bumper crop of grapes, and old-timers claim it's the vines reacting to a reduction of irrigation water.

Which brings me to the realization that my vines and trees and irrigation practices are abnormal to the region. There are no natural survival mechanisms triggered on my farm. Everything I do is manipulation. I can't expect a miraculous, truly natural farming system to automatically replace my old system. Wildflowers won't just grow when I start farming naturally. Likewise, my farm won't "naturally" solve its problems without my intervention.

When human beings first began to take care of a plant food source, instead of simply foraging and gathering, when a clan started tending its first berry patch, when farming was born, so was the manipulation of nature. Farmers all manipulate nature, some more than others. And some practices are more destructive than others. I may believe I can fool mother nature, but it's more as if she lets me get away with a few things. She'll naturally take care of her wildflowers and let me struggle with growing peaches and grapes in a desert.

THE YOUNG MAN had a bunch of wildflowers in his hand when I drove up. Golden poppies ringed his bouquet, lavender lupines stood erect in the center, with wild baby's breath and black-eyed Susans filling the rest. Next to his car were a box and some paper files. He proudly showed me his collection. He had just divided a dozen types of wildflowers and pressed them for his semester assignment.

"Your professor should be impressed. He'll think you hiked miles in the foothills for such a diverse collection," I said.

"I was lucky to find all of them here," he answered.

He wrapped his bouquet in newspaper, then began to gather the rest of his material. Even as he rolled down his car window to say goodbye, I kept waiting for him to say something about all the flowers he took from my vineyard. He waved and drove down the road, a probable *A* on his semester project sitting in the box next to him.

I stood motionless, dumbfounded and stunned. Didn't that boy wander through my fields? Didn't he know this land belonged to someone? Didn't he know someone planted and tended these lush cover crops? Didn't he just steal a hoard of flowers from my farm?

I talked with Marcy about my anger. She listened and then laughed.

"I don't think it's funny," I said.

"You just don't get it, do you?" she said. "The boy's class assignment was to gather a wildflower collection, and he did just that. . . . Remember, he found a field of 'wi-ii-ld' flowers."

ONE DAY MY neighbor asked me about my natural farming. For years he's driven by every day and watched my cover crops and "wild" farming methods. He asked about the wildflowers first.

"They're pretty," I commented.

"Yeah," he said, nodding, "Ann"—his wife—"keeps reminding me."

"It's taken awhile but they've finally established themselves," I said.

"You got them scattered all over."

"It's been awhile since I planted them."

"Wait." He perked up. "You mean you planted them?"

"Oh, yeah. It wasn't too hard. The seed was expensive, about twenty-five dollars a pound, but you get tens of thousands of seeds for that price."

He wasn't listening to my numbers. "You actually planted them?" he repeated.

"I broadcast them by hand, here and there."

"You mean, they didn't just start growing?"

I paused, unsure about his question. "Well, they took awhile to get established, the drought probably slowed them down." We both paused, and I sensed we were talking about two different things.

He turned as we heard Ann drive up the road. She pulled over and told me how pretty the wildflowers were.

"Thanks. I'll try planting some over near your driveway."

"You mean you plant them?" she asked.

"Sure."

"Oh." She smiled and repeated how much she liked passing them each day and drove off.

I repeated the conversation with Marcy that evening and she helped me clarify it. "They think the wildflowers just started growing once you began to farm naturally."

"They don't really believe that," I growled.

"Sure. Think about it. Natural farming and wildflowers, they're supposed to go together."

"You mean someone thinks that just because you start farming naturally, all the wonderful wildflowers automatically and magically grow, as if they've been dormant all these years just waiting for the day you stop using herbicides or chemicals? That day comes and magically the flowers appear?"

Marcy nodded her head, smiled, and said, "Well, didn't they?"

# chapter two

# workers of the land

## *Morning Porches*

From our porch I can survey the farm.

In front of our house live the oldest living creatures in the area, eighty-five-year-old grapevines with gnarled and twisted trunks, still producing tons of grapes despite their age. As the morning sun warms the air, the shoots of those old vines stretch to bathe new leaves in the light of day.

The dew sparkles in the early glow and I make plans. My list includes farmwork, family schedules, and things I hope to think about during the day. Farmwork provides many opportunities for contemplation, escapes from the tedious physical pace. I do my best thinking while shoveling weeds or driving a tractor.

I gaze at the fields and see the fragile vine shoots of early spring growth. They wave gently as if to remind me that they will soon require water. The peach blossoms are falling, the delicate pink petals dried and withered. Farmers call this period when the birth of the peach becomes visible "fruit set." Within weeks the peaches will double and triple in size and require hand thinning. I look to the west and monitor an advancing Pacific storm. Rain would save an irrigation but also create an ideal environment for mildew on my grapes and brown rot spores on my peaches.

From the porch I survey the years of work that contributed to the landscape before me. I scan the rise in the land to the southwest, an area that was once a small hill. Dad leveled the knoll but only after a year of removing hardpan rocks from the ground, stone after stone, load after load. Now there stands a healthy vineyard.

I recall the old red barn. The farmer before us had a small dairy and stored hay in that barn. But our forklift couldn't fit beneath the rafters, so Dad and I replaced it a few years ago with a new fourteen-foot-high pole shed. (I saved the cement slab that was once the floor of the milking parlor. Later I buried chunks of that concrete beneath the footings of my new porch addition.)

I can see my Sun Crest peaches. Every year more and more branches die from old age and wood borers. When I cut them out, the trees look funny, like a five-year-old's smile that's missing some teeth. I wonder if a new generation of healthy shoots will replace the lost wood.

My early morning view from the porch helps place me, a daily reminder of where I am. As I finish my cup of coffee and my plans for the day, I think of my family's past, the history of this valley, and the stories about these vineyards and orchards.

In the process of exploring the landscape I discover a little bit more of who I am.

## One Hundred Years of Farming

I'm a third-generation Japanese American farmer but am quite sure my lineage in agriculture dates back centuries. The Masumotos are from a solid peasant stock out of Kumamoto, Japan, rice farmers with not even a hint of samurai blood.

My grandparents journeyed from Japan to farm in California. They spoke Japanese instead of English or Spanish or German. They were Buddhists instead of Protestants, Catholics, or Jews. They came in 1898 and 1917 instead of the late 1700s or early 1800s. They sailed east instead of west, yet their voyage was similar to those of hundreds of thousands of other immigrants who crossed an ocean to the land of opportunity.

I farm the land my father and mother farmed, land where my grandparents probably labored as farm workers. My family is typical of the majority of farm families in California. We come from foreign soils to settle and work lands that have a relatively short history of cultivation. I know well the family who owned our farm before the Masumotos and can talk to some of the first pioneer farmers in the area. Agriculture in California is only a hundred years old.

Being only a hundred has its advantages. There is little history about how things were done. Even the old-timers were renegades of sorts. That's why they settled here, leaving some other place, pulling up roots, replanting themselves. They broke old traditions to establish new ones in California.

If there is any tradition in California, it is a tradition of innovational change. Our agriculture is founded on change, it grew and prospered with change, and it is banking on staying on the cutting edge. It is a precarious position. I can't very often say, "What worked for my father and his father will work for me." It's more like, "What worked a few years ago may still work today . . . but don't plan on its working tomorrow." I never met a farmer who wasn't trying something new to make work easier or to improve his land. All of which doesn't bode well for old-fashioned peaches.

During my college years at Berkeley, I'd occasionally visit home, finding comfort in the stability of life on the farm. Orchards and vineyards appeared the same, the farm seemed to remain just as I had left it. I was wrong, though, blinded by the naive perspective of the visitor.

In the last century, change in American agriculture was like a revolution, toppling old structures with new technologies, creating new products, new markets, and new farms. These forces pulled farmers along, some of us kicking and screaming, but innovation became the buzzword for success and survival.

My peaches are part of that cycle of change. They are part of a tradition on our farm, they hold meaning for my family. But the pressures for progress challenge that meaning. Am I overly sentimental about these peaches? How long do I cling to old definitions of quality? Does old also imply obsolete? I feel like an immigrant: the ways of the old country pull at me, while the opportunities of a new land beckon. My peaches are like the traditions of the homeland—you don't simply leave them behind, you carry them with you like historical baggage.

We farmers in California celebrate our one hundredth birthday. Like generations before me, I continue to dream about the old and the new, living and working in a rich culture of tradition and change. Perhaps my questions are not that different from the ones my grandparents asked when they pursued a new life on the edge of a continent.

## Squatting with Farmworkers

I cannot farm without farmworkers. My peaches and grapes demand an army of seasonal help. Throughout my farm's history wave after wave of laborers have journeyed here; different people from different lands have worked these fields.

I sometimes picture my farm as a battlefield with troops of people struggling with nature in a hundred-year war. Germans, Italians, Chinese and Japanese, Armenians, Filipinos, and Mexicans—their voices have sounded over this farm, their families have walked these rows. I picture them with hats pulled below their eyebrows casting a dark shadow on their faces. Over the decades their uniforms look alike: old pale shirts relegated to the fields, odd assortments of pants, some baggy and torn, others snug with faded colors from countless washings. Their skin is dark from the sun. Few are heavy or overweight, for field work is merciless on the unfit. They share a ghostly look, part of the hidden world of farm laborers who have brought nourishment to the nation's tables for generations.

I visit a nearby country cemetery and read the names on the headstones: Green, Brisco, Filgas, Bagdasarian, Silvas, Carrillo; some stones with Chinese characters scratched in cement and others with no name, only a number—8-14. I imagine these people in the fields, filled with hope and arriving with strong backs. They worked for low wages and helped create a green oasis in this desert landscape. My grandparents were part of the Japanese wave of immigrants at the beginning of this century. Now the majority of farm laborers are from Mexico or are Mexican Americans.

Some farmworkers are employed full time and earn good wages. Most arrive with the spring work and summer harvests;

then, as the leaves turn autumn colors, they become invisible again. The work is hard and the wages low but these folks need jobs.

I'm not sure where they go during the off season. Many venture back to Mexico and spend winters in their native villages, working and farming a family plot. Others embody images from Steinbeck's *Grapes of Wrath*. They follow the crops from early spring vegetables in Texas to California for most of the summer and complete the cycle in Washington, picking fall apples. Some farmworkers remain here, living as neighbors and friends, becoming members of the community.

Some folks lump all brown-skinned people together, referring to farmworkers as "those people" and blaming many of society's problems on them. "They" are illegal aliens on welfare, draining tax dollars, assaulting and violating American laws. And we farmers are somehow responsible for them. Because I am dark from my hours in the fields, I have been mistaken for "one of them" and have seen the ugly face of this prejudice.

I have also been accused by labor activists of being an exploiter. "Why don't you pay your workers more?" they challenge.

"I wish I could," I answer. "But tell me, are you willing to pay more for your fruits and vegetables?"

If the price of peaches kept up with car prices, I would not be writing an epitaph for my Sun Crests.

I ask those folks if they've ever considered the exploitation of urban laborers, the people who work behind closed doors in restaurant kitchens, mow lawns, or clean rooms and offices after hours.

"Or is agricultural exploitation worse because farmworkers are so easily seen?" I ask.

I struggle with all this in my thoughts—faceless laborers stooped over lush green fields, harvesting food for life. They

move systematically, like lumbering machines. I sometimes
think, Why don't we employ our high-technology know-how,
replace these workers, and end this oppressive work? Then I
realize that the crouched workers depend on this work and dis-
placing them from the land will not rid the world of their
hunger.

I DO NOT employ many workers. My farm remains small
enough for Dad and me to do most of the work ourselves, except for the pruning and harvesting.

Dad once warned me, "Once you start hiring a lot, you're not
just a farmer anymore."

When I began managing a crew of workers I understood
what he meant. I found myself spending the majority of my
time preparing for their arrival, supervising them, and fixing
problems that arose. I grew frustrated with my own lack of
productivity and became stressed by down time, such as when
a fifteen-man crew would stand around watching me try to
jump-start a tractor stuck in the field or change a flat tire on a
fruit-bin trailer.

With workers in my fields my daily rhythms shift, and instead of jobs and chores I think in terms of productivity and
costs. I talk about the farm in terms of expenses per acre, and
suddenly yields become the easiest aspect of my work to quantify. I don the hat of a farm manager, not a farmer.

At certain times, I do this willingly. In order to keep the farm
operating I must keep it profitable, and the cost of workers plays
a pivotal role in that equation. Suddenly saving peaches takes
on an additional burden: my farm also contributes to people's
livelihoods. Finding a home for Sun Crest peaches goes beyond
my individual back-to-nature pursuits. I do not farm this land
as a hobby.

My farming creates work.

MY WORKERS COME from many places in Mexico and live in small towns scattered throughout the valley. Del Rey, where many of them stay, is the nearest town to my farm. The estimated population is about 1,500, but during the summer harvest the town swells to twice that size. The workers live in rented rooms, small cramped boardinghouses, or hidden bungalows in converted garages and toolsheds.

I visit one of these apartments. The workers live in a small outbuilding behind my foreman's house. Some of the men are standing, others are crouching in a familiar squat.

My grandmother squatted that way, peasants I saw in South America squatted that way, old folks in rural Japanese villages did the same. It is a common-folk way of resting and a fine observation point from which to watch the world. It's the squat I use when I'm waiting, not for anything in particular but the waiting and resting that's part of farming.

Squatting evens out physical differences. Tall people and short ones become closer in height when squatting. You share with others a common point of view. Once you squat you have to think twice about getting up; you become conscious of choices and decisions. Squatting is a mark of country folk who have worked the land and whose legs are in excellent condition. You can't squat well if you are overweight, if your legs are used to sitting in chairs, or if you are lazy. I wonder if we've lost the art of squatting. In our fast-paced world today, we're too busy or think we're too good to squat.

On my visit to their home, I recognize two of the squatting workers who picked my peaches that morning. With beers in their hands, crushed cans lying next to them, one jumps up and waves me over to offer a beer. I am about to accept in a gesture of friendship, but somehow I can't. I know the price they pay for a six-pack of beer equals an hour of work. I calculate that a single beer equals picking one extra tree in 105-degree heat. I think of that worker earlier in the day, his sweat mingling with peach fuzz, his expression exhausted. I politely decline the drink and squat next to him.

I examine the workers' apartment, converted from a tool-shed or a freestanding single-car garage. I'm sure it isn't legal housing and I'm positive my foreman makes a good income from renting out the space. Yet I'm certain the workers are sat-isfied with finding any housing at all and with the protection they receive from my foreman, a good man who seems fair and quiet. He doesn't allow gambling, drugs, or prostitutes on his place. In fact, his own family lives in the adjacent house and one of his daughters is married to one of the steady workers. One farmworker tells me he has returned here for ten years, coming back to Mario's place every time. For these farmworkers, this is their shelter.

Inside the house are rows of bunks and a small kitchen, with a bathroom attached to the outside. One fellow is designated cook, and he explains how skillful he is at saving money and stretching the meat with beans and vegetables. The cook says he makes lunches for everyone who has work the next day. They pool their expenses. Some of my peaches are sitting on the counter to be shared. He finishes his beer, asks if I'd like a peach, and smiles. I can't tell if he's joking or not.

I am relieved to see that everything seems adequate and that my workers are being treated fairly. A lot of farmers do feel re-sponsibility for their workers. Most of the older farmers know from personal experience what it is like to work the land for low wages and to live in simple shelters.

As I leave, I think of the disparity between my home and the farmworkers' housing. I remember my first summer after col-lege at Berkeley. I wanted to solve the problems of poverty and inequality immediately. I adopted the popular idea of thinking globally and acting locally by doubling the prevailing wages for our workers. After calculating expenses and income for that month, I realized we had lost thousands of dollars. My idealism was then moderated. I concluded that providing jobs was the best contribution I could make to the world.

Now I try to pay a little better than the prevailing wage and I work out in the fields alongside the workers. And sometimes I still squat with them.

## The Lottery

A handful of lottery tickets scatter in the wind and drift into my peach orchard. I count over thirty of them, equaling more than half a day's wages for one man. Four hours of a man's labor and sweat, wasted and lost on a summer breeze.

The next day I ask about the tickets. A few of the workers smile and one razzes another. None of them has ever won more than five dollars.

Why do they keep playing *lotería*? Don't they understand the terrible odds against winning and the squandering of their hard-earned wages? Their answers are probably no different from those of anyone else who gambles, especially those whose lives are and will continue to be a struggle. They play for the chance to dream.

The California lottery payout nears a national record. We all feel the lotto fever, and I joke with the workers about it. They ask what I would do if I won. I say I'd quit farming and give them the farm tomorrow. One snaps back, "You can do that now without winning the *lotería*."

One of the farmworkers banters with me and says, "*Patrón* would never give us his farm."

I concede he is right.

"So," he adds, "if I win the *lotería,* I can buy your farm." The field roars with the work crew's laughter.

I don't play the lottery and cannot share the dreams of my workers. Occasionally when disking the peaches or grapevines, I'll find one of their losing tickets tossed among the leaves. The blades slice the paper and turn it into the earth, and for hours I'll think about lotteries and hope.

chapter three

# as if the farmer died

## Allowing Nature to Take Over

I used to have armies of weeds on my farm. They launch their annual assault with the first warm weather of spring, parachuting seeds behind enemy lines and poking up in scattered clumps around the fields.

They work underground first, incognito to a passing farmer like me. By the end of winter, dulled by the holidays and cold fog, I have my guard down. The weeds take advantage of my carelessness.

The timing of their assault is crucial. They anticipate the subtle lengthening of each day. With exact calculation they germinate and push upward toward the sunlight, silently rooting themselves and establishing a foothold. The unsuspecting farmer rarely notices any change for days.

Then, with the first good spring rain, the invasion begins. With beachheads established, the first wave of sprouting creatures rises to boldly expose their green leaves. Some taunt the farmer and don't even try to camouflage themselves. Defiantly they thrust their new stalks as high as possible, leaves peeling open as the plant claims more vertical territory. Soon the concealed army of seeds explodes, and within a week what had been a secure, clear territory is claimed by weeds. They seem to be everywhere, no farm is spared the invasion.

Then I hear farmers launching their counterattack. Tractors roar from their winter hibernation, gunbarrel-gray exhaust smoke shoots into the air, and cold engines churn. Oil and diesel flow through dormant lines as the machines awaken. Hungry for work, they will do well when let loose in the fields. The disks and cultivators sitting stationary throughout winter rains await the tractor hitch. The blades are brown with rust stains, bearings and gears cold and still since last fall. But I sense they too may be anxious to cleanse themselves in the earth and regain their sleek steel shimmer.

Even the farmers seem to wear peculiar smiles. Through the cold winter season, they were confined to maintenance, repairing equipment, fixing broken cement irrigation gates, replanting lost trees and vines. Their hibernation culminates with a desk assignment at the kitchen table, where they sit surrounded by piles of papers, laboring on taxes (farmers are required to file by March first). After restless hours of poring through shoe boxes of receipts and trying to make sense of instructions written by IRS sadists eager to punish all of us who are self-employed, farmers long for a simple task outside. We are anxious to walk our fields, to be productive, to work our land. A full winter's worth of pent-up energy is unleashed on the tiny population of weeds.

Within a day or two, the genocide is complete. Fields become "clean," void of all life except vines and trees. Farmers take no prisoners. I can sometimes count the number of weeds missed by their disks. "Can't let any go to seed," a neighbor rationalizes. Each seed becomes a symbol of evil destruction and an admission of failure.

Farmers also enlist science to create a legion of new weapons against the weeds. They spray preemergent herbicides, killing latent seed pods before they germinate. Others use contact or systemic killers, burning the delicate early growth of weeds and injecting the plants with toxins that reach down to the roots. As spring weeds flourish between rows, a strip of barren earth beneath each vine or tree magically materializes from a spray applied a month or two before. At times I wonder what else is killed in order to secure the area.

A weed might be defined as any undesirable plant. On my farm, I used to call anything that wasn't a peach tree or a grapevine a weed. I too considered a field clean if it contained nothing but dirt, barren of anything green except what I had planted. All my neighbors did likewise. We'd compete to see whose field would be the cleanest. But our fields weren't clean. They were sterile.

We pay a high price for sterility, not only in herbicide bills and hours of disking but also in hidden costs like groundwater contamination. Some farmers can no longer use a certain herbicide because the California Department of Agriculture tested and discovered trace residues contaminating the water tables beneath their farms. It had been widely used because it kills effectively and is relatively cheap; for about $10 per acre it would sterilize an entire field.

But signatures of a clean field can stay with the farm for years. Behind my house, I planted some landscape pines, hardy, cheap, grow-anywhere black pines—that kept dying. They died a slow death, the needle tips burning before turning completely brown, the top limbs succumbing first, the degeneration marching down toward the heartwood like a deadly cancer. Uncertain of the cause of death, I gave up trying to grow the pines after the third cremation. Staring at the barren area I at last discovered the reason: nothing grew on that strip of earth. The preemergent herbicide I once used remains effective and has left a long-term brand on the land.

But I now have very few weeds on my farm. I removed them in a single day using a very simple method. I didn't even break into a sweat. I simply redefined what I call a weed.

It began with an uncomfortable feeling, like a muse whispering in my ear, which led to an observation about barren landscapes. It doesn't make sense to try and grow juicy grapes and luscious peaches in sterile ground. The terms *juicy* and *luscious* connote land that's alive, green most of the year with plants that celebrate the coming of spring.

A turning point came when a friend started calling his weeds by a new name. He referred to them as "natural grasses." I liked that term. It didn't sound as evil as "weeds," it had a soft and gentle tone about it. So I came to think of my weeds as part of the natural system at work on my land, part of allowing nature to take over my farm.

And nature did take over. Once I let my guard down and allowed a generation of seeds to germinate, they exploded everywhere. For years I had deceived myself into thinking I had destroyed every weed seed. I was wrong, they were just waiting for an opportunity.

The first weed of spring is the pineapple weed, covering the vine berms. But it quickly wilts with the first heat of May.

Chickweed hugs every tree, growing into a lush mat before dying with the first 80-degree days. This grass may be allelopathic, producing toxins that kill competing weeds. Because few other plants grow through the mat, the yellowed and dry chickweed works like a protective mulch guarding the tree trunks.

By the middle of spring, the grasses flourish and a sea of weeds fills all but the sandiest and weakest earth. I try to keep my vine and orchard berms clear, a lesson gleaned from an earlier confrontation with a weed named mare's tail. This tall and slender creature can grow straight up into a vine leaf canopy and out the top. Mare's tail doesn't hurt vines, but at harvest the workers must battle the pollen and fight through a wall of stalks and leaves to reach the precious grapes. So I try and keep my new natural grasses away from the vine berms and tree trunks.

As nature takes over my farm, everything grows voraciously. New insect life swarms in my fields. Aphids coat sow thistle like pulsating black paint. Normally aphids aren't a problem for grapevines and peach trees, they would rather suck on sow thistle. But they are denied that meal because of the thousands of lady beetles that invade my fields for spring feasting. I wonder what other invisible life thrives in the natural grasses, what pathogens and parasites join my farm. I can't measure their presence but I feel secure, and the grapes and peaches still look fine.

I walk my fields and feel life and energy. In the evening a chorus of voices calls out, legions of insects venturing out to feed. On family bike rides we have to keep our mouths closed or bugs will fly in.

I often think, There's something going on out here, and smile to myself.

I was a fool to try to control weeds. I fooled myself by keeping fields sterile without knowing the long-term prices I was paying. Allowing nature to take over proved easier than I imag-

ined. Most grasses will naturally die back without my intervention, and I've learned to recognize those few that I should not
ignore. Most natural grasses are not as bad as farmers fear.

In the eyes of some farmers, my farm looks like a disaster,
with weeds gone wild. Even my father grows uncomfortable.
He farmed most of his life during an era of control, and to him
the farm certainly now appears completely chaotic. He keeps a
few rows next to his house weed-free as if to maintain a buffer
between him and a lifetime of nightmares from fighting
weeds.

I still have bad dreams about some obnoxious grasses like
Bermuda, but my nightmares ended once I stopped thinking of
them as weeds.

## Lizard Dance

While weeding, I feel something tickle my calf. Without stopping my shovel, I brush the back of my leg. It happens again and
I assume the clumps of johnsongrass I dug out are rolling off
their pile, the thick stalks and stems attacking their killer in a
vain attempt at revenge. Finally, I shake my right leg, and the
thing bolts upward.

Immediately I throw down my shovel and stamp my feet.
The adrenaline shoots into my system and my heart races. I initiate my lizard dance, shaking my leg, pounding my feet, pat-
ting my pants as the poor creature runs wild up my leg. The
faster I spin and whirl, the more confused the lizard becomes
and the more frantically he scrambles up and down the dark
caverns of my pant leg.

In the middle of my dance, I begin laughing, recalling the familiar feel of a lizard running up my pants, through my shirt,
and down my sleeves. My body dances uncontrollably to the feel

of its tiny feet and little claws grabbing my skin. I try to slow down, knowing the lizard will too if we both relax.

But as the creature scampers up higher and higher my imagination runs wild. Vulnerable body parts flash in my mind.

If other workers were around, they would laugh, watching me tug at my belt, frantically trying to drop my pants. With luck, I won't open a crevice in my shorts, inviting the lizard into another dark hiding place. Instead he'll be attracted to daylight, leap out of my crotch, and tumble to the ground, dazed for a moment before scampering into the safety of weeds and undergrowth.

I enjoy the return of lizards to my farm. They were plentiful in my youth, soaking up the rays of the sun, eating bugs and insects, living happily in the patches of grasses and weeds. Then we disked and plowed their homes and sprayed to kill most of their food. The lizards left.

I didn't plan on raising lizards, but they're part of a natural farm landscape. Besides, their presence reminds me of my childhood. I can't return to those days but I can try and foster new life on the farm, along with laughter and the lizard dance.

## Farming with Chaos

Chaos defines my farm. I allow natural grasses to go wild. I see new six-legged creatures migrating into my fields, which now look like green pastures. I watch with paranoid panic, wanting to believe all will be fine while terrified I may lose the crop and even the farm. I need a lesson on managing chaos.

The small town of Del Rey is two and a half miles from my farm. When Japanese immigrants first settled there in the early 1900s, one of the first structures erected was a community hall, a place for meetings, gatherings, dinners, and festivals, a refuge from the tough life in the fields. The grounds around the hall were never truly landscaped. The sparse collection of trees and shrubs was lost in droughts and freezes, taken out for a basketball court, or neglected during World War II, when all Japanese were forced to evacuate the West Coast, leaving the trees without a caretaker. But there are still a few trees and bushes at the old hall, sporadically cared for during community gatherings. At one of these meetings I was taught my first lesson on chaos.

Two old-timers were pruning one of the Japanese black pines. They were retired farmers and gardeners, a common dual profession for struggling farmers who found that they could supplement their income by tending other people's gardens. The two old men worked in silence as they clipped away, pulling off needles and shaping the tree. The pine was not an eighty-year-old bonsai masterpiece. It was probably something left over from one of their gardening jobs, an extra pine donated to the hall perhaps fifteen years ago and gradually shaped and pruned.

I asked if I could help. They both nodded without looking up and kept working. I waited for some direction but they kept probing the bottom of each limb, stopping at a small outgrowth and quickly snapping it off. Their fingers gently raked the branches, tugging and separating unwanted growth. Their glassy old eyes wandered across the needles, stopping and guiding clippers, then moving on, scanning and studying the tree.

"How do you know what to cut?" I asked. One glanced up and smiled softly. His entire face seemed to mold around the grin as if all the wrinkles worked in unison to accommodate the gesture. A smile was familiar to that face.

I repeated my question and he whispered something in Japanese I could not hear or understand. They both returned to their clipping and snipping. The next time, just as he cut a small branch, I pointed and asked, "Why did you cut that one?"

He looked up as if wakened from a trance and blinked. "*Saa* . . . I don't know." He returned to his work.

I was relegated to watching their movements, trying to guess why they cut or passed on a branch, why some needles were pulled and thinned and others weren't. Their hands massaged the pine, their eyes wandering up and down a scaffold as fingers stroked and probed the interior of the tree. I tried with my hands but was quickly entangled in decisions. When do you leave a new branch and for how long? What was the rule when pruning? What are the criteria for cutting? I was overlooking something very basic, something I couldn't see in front of me.

The pine was only maintained once or twice a year. It had a wild quality about it, unlike the meticulously tended backyard Japanese garden variety. It was a living chaos, a reflection of the natural ebbs and flows of erratic irrigations, unprotected frosts and heat waves, and inconsistent care from an aging ethnic farm community. Yet out of this uncontrolled growth, these two old-timers were sculpting a beautiful tree, simple and innocent.

I never did grasp the art of pruning that pine tree. Later, during a summer heat wave, when the farmers were all out desperately trying to get water to thirsty grapes and trees, one of the hall's pine trees died. (I also learned that both old men had acute hearing problems and probably hadn't heard any of my questions.) But as I try to farm more naturally, I keep thinking of those two farmers and their dancing hands. They had no secret pruning method. Perhaps there is no secret to farming and managing chaos—you blend tradition and science with some common sense and trust you'll have a crop. In fact, most good farmers I know are like those two old men, tending to their trees and vines as best they can, comfortable with their work, and confident that the final product will be fine. Whether they know it or not, seasoned farmers are already experts at chaos.

## As If the Farmer Died

This year I've abandoned my old farmwork schedules, which were often set by the calendar. I have no set mowing program or irrigation timeline. I devote more hours to monitoring my fields, and I curb my impulse to find quick fixes. Not only can I identify the pests that are munching on my fruits, I also recognize when they don't seem to be doing any more damage than usual. I'm learning to live with them, realizing that I've probably always had these pests but never scrutinized the farm so closely. I monitor the weeds as they creep up to new heights and discover some I have never seen before. I watch for new lush growth and wonder if the compost I added last fall is working. Each day I accumulate impressions more than lessons, as I develop the instincts of those two old farmers.

I used to farm with a strategy of un-chaos. I was looking for regularity, less variability, ignoring the uniqueness of each farm year. But now my farm resembles the old pine at the Del Rey Hall; wildness is tolerated, even promoted. The farm becomes a test of the unconventional, a continuous experiment, a journey of adaptation and living with change. I've even had to change my ways of counting. It's no longer important how *many* pests I have, what matters is the ratio between good bugs and bad bugs. I try to rely less and less on controlling nature. Instead I am learning to live with its chaos.

During the evenings my family sits on the porch and we listen to the songs of the insects, a chorus of new voices. I walk through my orchards and watch squadrons of flying insects swarming above the cover crops, chasing each other before dive-bombing into trees. During moments of insecurity, I still have occasional anxiety attacks and threaten to call in the bulldozer and regain order, to rid myself of these tumultuous peaches that just taste too damned good.

I can't hide my experiments and failures. Neighbors drive past, watch my progress, and talk with my wife while my weeds grow, seemingly out of control. They ask if something has happened to me.

My farm looks as if the farmer has died.

*chapter  four*

# new farm, old pests

## Abunai Kusa: *Dangerous Grass*

Most of my peaches and grapes are grown without herbicides.
As a result, I've learned a lot about weeds and can identify most
of them by name. I have developed a friendship with some,
while others continue to fool me.

Most I no longer consider weeds. I call them "indigenous
growth" (it sounds more scientific than "natural grasses") and
try to ignore them. The majority disappear quickly, dying in the
summer heat. Others only require a quick pass with a blade,
their shallow roots easily submitting to my tractor and weed
cutter.

But there are a few that remain weeds. One is johnsongrass. When I see that weed, I can't help but think of my *baachan,* my grandmother. She called johnsongrass by a special name, *abunai kusa. Abunai* means dangerous and *kusa* means grass: dangerous grass.

She called it dangerous not because it was poison to humans but rather because it was poison to a farm. Johnsongrass is a voracious grower and spreads rapidly and deeply. Uncontrolled, it grows and monopolizes sunlight, suffocating vines and choking roots. It is almost impossible to kill johnsongrass. The only means of control is to chop off the stalks and stems and dig up as much of the roots as you can. Even then, when the new sprouts emerge, you have to repeat the process.

"You can't ignore them," Baachan said. "They dangerous. *Abunai.*"

And to a struggling farmer they *are* dangerous. The land means everything, and johnsongrass is a poison, a special poison to the land.

New herbicides can now kill johnsongrass easily. When my grandparents farmed, they had a different relationship not only with the land but also with their weeds. Some weeds were indeed *abunai,* and I realize they can remain dangerous for my peaches, my farm, my family—my dreams.

## Cooking Bermuda

I found a way to kill Bermuda weeds without an herbicide or destroying my back. All it requires are a tractor, fuel, and time. Farmers may have tractors and fuel, but time is becoming increasingly rare.

I discovered this system quite by accident. In one block of vines where I did not use herbicides, I had to experiment with alternatives in order to control a small patch of Bermuda. Dad told me to watch Bermuda like a hawk. He warned, "Once it's established you have to work doubly hard to destroy it." For my father and his generation, that sort of intensive labor was work; my generation considers it purgatory. The thought of doubling my efforts lodged in my mind and translated into hours of shoveling and a sore back.

I recall seeing Baachan as she stooped over a shovel, working her hands, pulling stubborn roots, slicing and stabbing the weeds, leaving a series of small piles of drying turf behind her. For hours she'd work, then stand and trudge home for lunch, leaning forward as if walking against the wind, her back bent and shoulders hunched.

My God, I thought, that's why all those old folks from farm villages walked that way. It wasn't just age, it was from hours stooped over a shovel. It was from Bermuda. I was determined to find a different way to attack my weeds.

I found a compromise position between the generations. I kill Bermuda by disking it again and again and again and alternate that with days where the 100-degree heat does the work for me, cooking the nasty weed.

Bermuda poisons a farm. I read that it was allelopathic, like chickweed, literally carrying a noxious poison as it spreads, killing competitors in its path. Bermuda grows as a thick mat, and once it is rooted you can barely cut it with a shovel. Even then, you will probably miss a portion that will lie dormant underground until life-giving water comes along and presto, the green will return with new sprouts and shoots.

Herbicides work well against Bermuda. Some burn like a liquid fire, searing the weed's green leaves and stems. Others kill in a systemic fashion. Sprayed on green growth, the chemical is absorbed into the cells and destroys the roots, making it more efficient and less toxic than other methods. But as part of my decision to farm a different way, I chose not to use chemical controls for my fields. When an herbicide kills weeds, I wonder, what other life dies? Part of my desire in saving my Sun Crest peaches is to build, not destroy life.

A few summers ago I was preparing the ground for the coming fall and dormant season. Many farmers make a final pass through their fields, disking in the last of the summer weeds, turning the earth over for winter beds.

In one row I discovered a small stand of Bermuda growing in the middle of the row, thick and matted. It looked like a putting green, a manicured oasis in the rough. I made a pass over it with the disk, and the blades simply bounced on the turf. I stopped, backed up, and made another pass. The blades followed the same path and gradually began slicing into the tight mass of grass and roots. I repeated the process over and over, and with each effort my disk cut deeper until I actually turned over fat slices of sod. I thought of selling the Bermuda logs to new homeowners as instant landscaping: "Guaranteed. Just add water."

Because the Bermuda row happened to be along my driveway, I could monitor any weed rebirth. A few days later I noticed something green. The turf logs had rerooted and new Bermuda shoots were searching for sunlight. It was returning like a creature in a bad horror movie.

The disk was still connected to the tractor so I vented my anger on the putting green, which had now become a small golf range. All I accomplished was to spread the Bermuda down the row, doubling its territory. So I repeated the purging and once again pulverized the turf. Since the roots were already sliced, they gave way more easily this time. I diced them into small chunks yet feared I had only replanted a longer fairway.

Then nature came to my rescue. A heat wave visited the valley and daytime temperatures soared into the 100s. The diced Bermuda baked and fried. I returned to the patch and found almost all the life sucked from the roots. The small chunks of turf broke up in my hands. With a final disking the Bermuda cleansing was complete. The roots were cooked, the humus soft, like powder.

Yet I knew some roots bury themselves deep in the earth and will resprout next year. I imagined they would become a small archipelago, strung out along the vine row. I marked the spot with bright yellow surveyor's tape and planned to return for an annual purge.

I discovered a system not much different from my father's and my grandmother's. They too would return to the same spot year after year, attacking the Bermuda. I have revived the old practice, albeit with a modern 65-horsepower tractor. Even with my "new" traditional approach to farming, quick fixes are rare and a good memory may be my best ally against weeds. I have a competitive friendship with my Bermuda, and I return to it annually. Some years I have to give ground, other times I gain the upper hand. But I come back again and again, thinking of time in terms of years, perhaps even a lifetime.

However, the tractor poses an organic farming paradox: I may not use herbicides but I burn huge amounts of fuel and energy on a relatively small block of weeds. I sometimes think, One good shot of herbicide and the Bermuda could have been taken care of for years. Meanwhile billows of diesel exhaust trail behind my tractor with each assault. So I think about air pollution as I farm "naturally." I feel a little guilty until I think of Baachan's strong back and her tenacity to battle weeds, neither of which I possess. I sense my paradox will not be resolved soon.

## Sprinting and Spring Peaches

Dad doesn't believe in early season peaches. "They not natural," he says. "That's why we plant mid-season ones like Sun Crest."

Dad's orchards were always harvested in the heat of summer, his peaches well suited for the 100-degree days and the fine sandy loam of our farm. Dad knows the land and didn't try to push mother nature.

I ignored his advice and planted five acres of an early variety of peach called Spring Lady. They bloom in March and are harvested by May, seventy days to evolve from blossoms into luscious fruit. They challenge nature's clock, genetic mutations racing against natural timelines.

I tried to rationalize my decision to Dad. "Spring peaches may be unnatural for the valley, but people buy lots of peaches in May. They pay good prices."

He stood unmoved.

I continued. "We'll just be nudging mother nature a little. Besides, making money shouldn't be an unnatural act for a farmer."

He shook his head and, like a good parent, left me to learn the hard way.

My first error was planting the Spring Ladies in the wrong ground. This field has "light soil," a euphemism for poor, sandy dirt. It will take years to build up the earth and enrich it with nutrients, organic matter, and humus.

I shared my plight with one of my workers, an older Mexican fellow with more experience in the fields than I will ever have. His comments become useful in such situations. Shrugging his shoulders and raising his eyebrows, he said, "What can you do?"

For the first two years of the orchard, I aborted the crop, channeling all the energies into growth. Without a harvest, I paid little attention to the young field, ignoring the weak trees. By the third year the young trees were flush with pink blossoms. Yet for some reason, many of the trees had trouble growing leaves. My other peach varieties rapidly grow with the first spring warmth. The fields change from the pink of blossoms to a pale green of fresh shoots. My Spring Ladies progressed from bright pink to a faded red of withering petals. Tiny oval peaches eventually emerged as the bloom fell and blanketed the earth with a sanguine hue. And yet, despite their beauty, there was a problem: how could peaches grow without leaves? A few weeks later a few shoots appeared and I began to relax, reassured Spring Lady was not some new leafless variety.

Later in the spring I hired thinners to enter my orchards and destroy over half the Spring Lady crop. They climb ladders and knock off thousands of the tiny peaches with their fingers. The earth is covered with these little peach corpses, they crunch beneath your feet as you walk. The sound of a crew thinning peaches reminds me of a thunderstorm, the falling fruit knocking against ladder steps and pattering on the ground, building from a light tapping to a dazzling crescendo as the crew picks up speed.

Good farmers don't look down during thinning; the sight of the thousands of bodies would trouble their thoughts. Too easily I translate fallen fruit into lost profits and I'm tempted to leave more on each tree, which actually results in lots of small, low-priced fruit. Once, while thinning, a crew boss waved his hands upward and told me, "Look up! Look up! Good farmers look up!" He sounded like both a good manager and a good therapist.

I shielded my eyes from the ground and concentrated on the Spring Lady thinners and their spacing of the fruit on a branch. I opted not to gamble and to leave only a single peach per hanger, or stem, about two hundred peaches per tree.

Every year the beauty of spring is interrupted by the work demands of vineyards and orchards. Spring work envelops the farmer. We run from one job to another, desperately trying to keep up with the pace of change. As the weather warms, the weeds surge, mildew spores multiply, insects munch, and roots need water. Small weeds rapidly mutate into thickets that challenge my largest disk and tractor. Fungi spread throughout my fields, spores hope to avoid detection, and, if unchecked, they multiply geometrically. Weak soils refuse to help struggling trees, and their tiny peaches are stunted without the intervention of some type of fertilizer. The race quickly turns into a sprint.

By the middle of April, with only a little over a month away from harvest, my first Spring Lady peaches were still the size of dried prunes. Dad is right, I thought, I can't fool nature. But the old Mexican worker was correct too. The trees were planted, I had a crop hanging, and so, "What can I do?"

My options were limited. A fertility program of compost would take months, if not years, to have an effect. I craved a quick fix, a steroid for peaches. They have one for grapes called gibberellic acid, a growth hormone modeled after a natural enzyme in grapes. But there isn't one for peaches.

I could experiment with a foliar feed, which pumps up the peaches, sort of like quick-acting vitamins. Some farmers have success with micronutrients, applying magnesium, sulfates, zinc, and calcium directly onto leaves. Others promote elixirs ranging from soup mixes of assorted natural elements like dried blood, fruit wax, bat guano (the catalog said "soak in water and use as guano tea"), and—the standby of organic gardeners—fish emulsion.

Perhaps because I am Japanese I seem to have an affinity for the seaweed-kelp foliar feeds. Kelp contains high levels of minerals, vitamins, enzymes, and natural-growth hormones and is world famous, at least that's how the brochure describes it. An advertisement from a different company promotes the "natural additives" of another concoction that includes Icelandic kelp (as opposed to Norwegian), molasses, coconut oil, garlic, onion, yeast, and more.

I began mixing the kelp and it smelled terrible. I hesitated before pouring it into my sprayer, envisioning five acres of beautiful fruit, each peach tasting slightly of seaweed. Could I market my fruit as an "oriental" variety, a rediscovery of the Asian roots of the original peach? But as it blended with the five hundred gallons of water in the tank, only a light green tinge stained the water.

I hoped to cover the entire tree—leaves, bark, and tiny fruit—with a gentle mist that coated the surface like a fog embracing the tree. While I was spraying, the breeze shifted and the mixture wet my face. I felt a tingling, probably more from the cold water and the cool spring temperatures than the seaweed. But as I felt the air brushing my cheeks and the chill of the moisture on my back, I knew I was sprinting.

With the short growing season, a slight mistake and a stumble and I'm out of the race. A contradiction as I try to work with nature? But isn't farming a compromise with nature? The day the first farmer stopped hunting and gathering and planted a seed, the contest was begun.

The best farmers know how to coax nature, massage and nudge her along. With seaweed sprays I could neutralize the negative effects of light soils and hope to make amends for selecting the wrong peach variety. The ultimate answer might be to bulldoze my Spring Lady trees and plant something that better matches my farm. But an interim solution might be to keep building my soils, hoping that eventually good earth would compensate for human errors and I could stop micromanaging with Band-Aid foliar sprays.

In May we harvested good Spring Lady peaches. They grew to a nice full size, and the market prices justified all the extra work. I felt a sense of accomplishment, proving to the world that I could grow decent early peaches despite my light ground.

I still believe that Sun Crest peaches are the perfect crop for my soils and climate, and their flavor and sweet juices just confirm that belief. Yet when I stare at my Spring Lady orchard, I see a world full of farmers sprinting with their fruits. We think nudging nature along can't hurt, and, after all, what's so bad about making a little money early in the season?

## Zen and the Peach Twig Borer

It hatches with the first warmth of spring and immediately seeks virgin green leaves. It begins feeding, munching on tender foliage and fattening its dirty-white body. Within days it will bore into a delicate green shoot, mining the fiber, carving a home out of the tissue, hiding from predators, gnawing and growing.

I've never seen the hatching of a peach twig borer. They're as tiny as a sliver and emerge in the tops of the peach trees. But I see signs of their work: tips of shoots dry out from their dining, tendrils turn brown and wither, hanging lifeless, dangling in the spring breeze. If I'm lucky, the worm is still inside, but most often the dead shoot is seen only after the creature has left to pupate elsewhere. In a few weeks it will emerge as an adult moth, laying eggs for the next invasion.

The aroma of a ripening peach lures caterpillars to its juicy nectar. They creep to the hanging fruit and gorge themselves, their bodies grow fat and change color, their bulbous flesh transmutes into brown and white rings. They feed on the surface, nibbling on the skin before gouging hunks out of the meat. They leave a crater where rot and mold find shelter. Some fruit will begin to bleed, juice oozing from the surface and dripping on leaves and other maturing fruit below. A stream of decay spreads from the wound.

The assault begins when a first generation of peach twig borers appears in early spring. By June a second generation is born, followed by another generation and then another. With the summer heat and long days, they multiply in shorter intervals, discovering a wonderful abundance of green shoots for homes, boring into the twigs and munching on fresh peaches during their summer picnics.

A few summers ago I discovered a peach twig borer invasion at harvesttime. My first bags of fruit were picked and dumped into large wooden harvest bins three feet deep. I reached in to taste my first juicy peach of the early morning and the fruit gushed in my hand. It can't be overripe yet, I thought. Then I turned it over and shuddered. The back side had been gouged, the peach violated; rot festered in the wounds. I picked up another and another, only to discover pockmarks strewn across the pink and red flesh.

I immediately inspected another bin, praying the infestation was isolated to one tree. The second bin was better, only about 10 percent of the fruit was damaged. Frantically I began tossing out the fruit, leaning into the bin, shoveling out dregs, purging the diseased. I panicked, wanting to destroy the evidence, to cleanse my fields.

I was in denial, and with justification. Should marketers learn of my affliction, they would scrutinize all my fruit, searching for more damage. I imagined my name blacklisted on brokers' desks, a thick red WORMS stamped across invoices.

But it was hopeless. I had a cancer. The fruit packers would cull heavily and produce brokers would be wary. I would help no one by trying to sneak a few extra fruits past inspection, only to learn that in a distant city someone bit into my peach and discovered the proverbial worm poking its head out of the fruit. The only worse nightmare would be if they found half a worm, and I'd have to claim that the peach twig borer is a surface feeder, so it couldn't be my worm. But that would not alter the hysteria. I still had worms.

Most worms usually are taken care of by spraying. Many farmers use a chemical in the winter that provides control for months, a worm toxin that destroys eggs and caterpillars during the cold temperatures. The spray also kills most everything else in the field. By early spring those orchards are sterile of life; lady beetles and lacewings avoid the area, repulsed by a natural quarantine of residues and the fact that there is no food for their hungry appetites.

Some of these chemicals are now prohibited. One university study revealed that, in damp moist conditions, droplets from a winter spray can travel great distances. Chemical particles become suspended in the air and ride the air currents. Our valley is susceptible to this kind of acid fog that drifts from field to field. I conjure overblown images of radioactive clouds rolling across the countryside, hovering above children in school playgrounds, marching toward suburban tracts. The study proved our sprays don't stop at property lines. Suddenly what a neighbor might do affects you more than you imagined. Having good neighbors is more important than ever.

Damage from peach twig borer occurs inconsistently. I've seen years when spray programs didn't work and my neighbors scratched their heads wondering why. I've also heard pest control advisers who sell farmers their chemicals explain the damage with the claim, "It was a wormy year." No one has proven that borers have developed a resistance to chemicals, but I've learned never to underestimate the ability of pests to adapt.

Bill, a friend and University of California researcher, is developing a new method to attack peach twig borers. He is a veteran of many years of battles, having seen the industry change with the deluge of new chemicals and sprays that have been developed since World War II. In the late forties and fifties, the nation shifted a wartime industrial complex from the European and Pacific fronts to my farm. I can imagine the nation's consciousness: "We beat the Germans and Japanese, why not go after insects next?"

Bill is exploring a novel idea: Why not use a less toxic treatment on the peach twig borer? Not fewer sprays but different ones. He advocates using a bacterium called *Bacillus thuringiensis,* or BT for short. Worms eat the BT and die, but the poison is very selective, leaving natural enemies and people unharmed. The major problem with these bacteria is their short life—they last only a few days in the field. Timing is therefore crucial. The spray must be applied precisely when the caterpillars are emerging.

I picture the peach twig borer making a mad dash for a green shoot, and in that window of opportunity I must apply my BT spray. It would be like those hundreds of little turtles that hatch and make a mad dash for the ocean, only to be snatched up by gulls and other critters. Must I be a gull, hovering above the beach front, patiently waiting for the hatch? Timing like that doesn't seem possible.

But Bill has a plan: spray early in the life of a peach twig borer while they're still young and much more vulnerable to a minute amount of poison. The idea is to use BT before the peach shoots are very long, when the worms are feeding on small leaves. Also BT will last a little longer in the cooler spring weather, when there are fewer leaves to coat with the bacteria and the worms are more exposed. Bill's plan is to lengthen the beach, so to speak, to shift the odds in favor of the farmer. But I will still have to time the spray with the hatch.

A realization: I don't understand the life cycle of the peach twig borer. For years I have killed it without thinking. But if I hope to raise my peaches organically and battle pests differently, I need to learn more about the life in my field, including the pests. I have never seen a peach twig borer infant worm. I hear they hatch in the tops of trees and somehow crawl to their first meal. But no farmer I know has ever seen a newborn borer.

Pat, a graduate student from the University of California at Berkeley, was completing his doctorate in entomology. We became friends and talked for hours about politics and farming. Walking through my orchards I often joked about our height differences; he was almost a foot taller. I claim that, at six feet four inches, Pat can see into the trees much more easily than I can, literally providing a different perspective on my peaches. His dissertation subject: "Peach Twig Borer."

We slip into hour-long conversations about this worm. I ask questions only a true scientist would get excited about, and he gently educates me with terminology a nonresearcher would understand. I demand he not use Latin on my farm. He explains to me the life cycle of the peach twig borer, its habits and characteristics. I ask questions about the borer's lifestyle: "What does it like to eat, when, and where?" He ponders for a moment, digesting my use of the term *lifestyle*. At times we digress into philosophical conversations: "Which came first, the peach or the peach twig borer?" Sometimes the questions develop into constructive dialogue about adaptation of a species and life biology.

My favorite question is: "When does the peach twig borer know when it's time to hatch?" Pat pauses, wondering if I'm asking some type of trick Zen question. I try again: "What triggers the hatching mechanism in the peach twig borer? If it hatches in the middle of winter, it will freeze. If it hatches with the first leaves, it will have a food source. If it hatches when there's lots of leaves, I don't have a prayer of nailing it with BT."

For once Pat doesn't have an immediate answer. The farmer stumps the scientist—and I grin. First he mumbles something about temperature and collects himself, then he corrects me. "Peach twig borers don't hatch, they overwinter in trees as very small caterpillars *in hibernaculum* and—" He stops when my face contorts with his Latin. "They hibernate in tiny cells that look like miniature chimneys," Pat continues, back on pace. He rambles about monitoring "temperature degree days" or the number of warm spring days until the first borer hatches, all of which sounds like a scientific method that takes all the fun out of the miracle of life and birth. Finally he counters, "Well, how do peaches know when to bloom?"

I answer with silence.

Still, I could not visualize the peach twig borer and sense that my run-for-life-to-the-ocean metaphor doesn't apply. But Pat has monitored some hatches and noticed that the new green shoots were too short for the worm to drill into. The hatch seems to be timed with the blooms and first leaves, before the first shoots grow beyond an inch or two. Perhaps a beachhead battle plan is appropriate.

Bill first mentions the term in a passing conversation. I corner him at a University of California agricultural field day, where researchers parade their projects to farmers. Actually the farmers are paraded around the 160-acre research station on vineyard wagons (pulled by tractors) from field to field, where a different scientist waits with bullhorn and a few charts and his research project tucked in the orchard behind him. I think of the old Soviet Union's October parades, with the generals standing as an arsenal of military hardware passes in review, only I'm not sure if the farmers are the generals or if we are the tanks and missiles.

I ask Bill about the spring arrival of the peach twig borer. He repeats what Pat taught me: peach twig borers overwinter in the tops of the trees and emerge in early spring, with the first leaves and shoots.

"They immediately bore into the shoots?" I ask.

"Well, no. There's not enough leaf growth for them," Bill answers.

My run-for-the-ocean image collapses.

Then Bill casually adds, "For those first days they wander. If there aren't many leaves they'll even eat blossoms, nibbling at them. They just graze until the shoots are long enough to bore into."

Graze. Peach twig borer grazing. I picture the worms slowly crawling out of their winter chimney homes, stretching, then making their way to their first good meal in months. They smell the pink blossoms, sense the fresh green leaves, and start their spring picnicking. After spending a winter cooped up in tiny sawdust mounds, they enjoy a few days out in the fresh air. So they graze, munching on some leaves, taking in some sun, listening to the spring birds, doing lunch with a dessert of peach blossoms.

I explain my vision to Pat and he smiles. Now I can see the peach twig borer and understand how a simple treatment of BT can work. Later I spray the bacteria onto the leaves, the tiny but hungry caterpillars gorge themselves, and the stomach poison does its job. Even if BT lasts only for a few days, the borers keep grazing, slowly feasting on a suicidal diet.

"They kill themselves," I claim. I grin at Pat and raise my eyebrows. He blinks, surprised at the look in my eyes. "It's the perfect crime," I conclude.

# chapter five

# learning to fail

## Shovel of Earth

The blade slices into the soil. My muscles tense and push the shovel into the moist ground. Dark and damp, the sweet warm smell of wet earth. The tool eases through a mat of weeds, the ground flush with activity. The metal face slides partially in, the soil is heavy and gently resists. Roots extend deep into an underground tangled mass beyond my sight.

I can't count the thousands of shovelfuls of earth I have moved in my life. But I like to think of the thousands that lie in my future, if I am fortunate.

Spring irrigation brings life to the orchards and vineyards. Peaches ripen and the scent of bloom lingers in the air. The vine buds push and the pale green of fresh growth emerges pure and delicate. My shovel blade pierces the earth again and again. I guide the water into my fields in an act of renewal, a confirmation of one more season.

The work frees my mind. Each shovel of the heavy, dank earth nurtures my soul with meaning about this place. My thoughts wander—to images of work to feed the soil, of harvests to feed the thousands. My labor renews the spirit as fields become invigorated with life.

Another spring unfolds.


## Changing Shades of Green

Pat and I walk my farm. We are an odd couple: he's trained as a scientist and an entomologist, I'm a farmer with a degree in sociology and rural studies. We compare what we see on the farm, but what's more important is what we don't see.

I've walked these fields thousands of times, he's entered hundreds of orchards. Oddly, those facts interfere with our perspectives, for we sometimes overlook the obvious. We both agree that walking may be the best management tool for farmers and researchers. Nothing replaces the personal and intimate sensibility of walking a farm, feeling the earth, seeing and smelling an orchard. But it's getting harder and harder to walk. Walking takes precious time, we can't cover a lot of ground, and first we have to break old habits and relearn the very act of walking.

I remember watching my children take their first steps. Walking was far more than a physiological task of muscle control and balance; it was driven by something inside, a motivation to explore. Adults often think of walking as merely a function of getting from one place to another, the start and finish is all that matters. But for children, a new dimension bursts open when they start walking, a new world of motion, of adventure, of discovery. They see a new world when they learn to walk.

Pat and I try to re-create our first steps into an orchard and see what's really in front of us, to capture the magical innocence of children and their endless curiosity about a new world. We wander through familiar workplaces with no questions in mind, attempting to walk without a destination.

"It's slow," I warn Pat.

"Almost painful," he adds.

As we leave the farmhouse porch and head toward the Sun Crest peaches, we agree to think out loud and share observations. Pat comments about my small five- and ten-acre blocks of vineyards, with dirt avenues dividing the fields. My equally small parcels of peach trees rise above the vines and break the horizon line. Other farms have been replanted in large forty- or eighty-acre sections, solid blocks of vines and trees. We both try to envision my farm from the sky, I imagine it looks like a patchwork quilt with a green appliqué.

"Think my small field size makes a difference?" I ask.

"It might," he says.

We allow ourselves to explore the topic. I can see him thinking of the possibilities: the advantages of mixed habitat for beneficial insects, the rich diversity of species, the problems of monocropping and the spread of pathogens or pests. I interrupt his mental calculations. "Small fields mean if I screw up in one, I only mess up a little." We smile. It's so easy to get too technical about this farming game.

We approach the Sun Crest orchard, and I focus on the weakest tree. Daily I pass this spot and am reminded of its frail condition. "I can't figure out what's the matter with that tree. It just doesn't like me," I comment.

"What tree?" Pat says and grins.

Pat slowly pans the entire field. Then he crouches to peer down a row. I join him. "Ever notice the changing shades of green?" he says.

I think of Paul, a farmer and oil painter friend. He enjoys experimenting with green, capturing the subtle nuances of a fresh leaf or the thriving growth of mid-spring or the weak yellow green of a cover crop on bad soil. When a group of us visit Paul's house, the farmers tend to gather around certain paintings. Paul knows his paintings work when we gravitate toward a few, attracted by the colors, and begin talking about his greens. The true green of a field has depth, like the mysterious colors of a clear but deep lake. Each shade has meaning we all interpret differently. Paul says farmers are his best art critics, we know of more greens than anyone else.

Pat and I enter the field. Sounds envelop us, birds call and sing, insects buzz and flutter. Each step sounds distinct. Underfoot lies a rough collection of stalks and stems, sticks and twigs, leaves and wildflowers. Diversity dwells in my fields.

We both experiment with the mechanics of walking and looking. I crouch low, feeling like an imitation Native American in my desperate effort to be one with nature. I try listening to my footsteps and establish a deliberate, methodical cadence that forces me to go slower. It's uncomfortable. I compare it to riding in a car with someone who drives with excruciating caution.

I hear myself breathing and discover a type of efficiency in movement. With a slow, patient stride, I can check the vigor of the cover crop, the dryness of the soil, the health of the leaves. I begin to notice the slumping peach shoots where a worm has struck, the different shades of green where mites establish their home. Instead of making three or four different checks of a field for specific pests or problems, I find I can get an impression of the whole orchard in one visit. This means decisions will be easier to make.

I turn to ask my companion how he's doing. I discover he's on the other side of the field. He looks dazed, without direction, almost expressionless, and I realize I must appear exactly the same.

I try to move even more slowly, turning my head from left to right, right to left, consciously panning the orchard. After a while my method seems to work, I begin to see hints of color I had overlooked. The younger limbs, perhaps only a few years old, push vibrant green shoots, the hue is light, and the surface appears shiny. Growth on the old thick branches seems darker and duller. Then I realize that the two sets of leaves are not the same age. The green on the established branches is maturer, with longer, more developed shoots, while not only do the young limbs have newer shoots but the nodes are closer together. The vibrant green may be a result of denser growth.

I'm not sure this makes a difference, but I do know that, on the same tree, peaches from old branches will ripen days earlier than those on younger limbs. Dad claims that old-growth peaches taste sweeter, but I've always thought he had an affinity for the old wood.

Tiny peaches cling to the slender limbs, and I catch myself envisioning them a few months from now at harvesttime. Two or three old branches do not look right, and I sense they may die before harvest. My conclusion is based only on a hunch that comes from having worked with these trees for decades. The trees provide subtle clues in a grand mystery that can alternately frustrate and torment or amaze and initiate.

I hear steps behind me. Pat is smiling. "We're getting the hang of it," he says, breaking the spell.

We continue to walk in silence. Then he turns.

"I'm sorry but I just can't help it." He pulls out a small hand lens dangling around his neck. "I've been trained as an ento-mologist for too long. I have to revert to my old ways." I give my approval, thankful he doesn't ask what I was just thinking. My thoughts have wandered too. I am calculating how many boxes of fruit I can pull from this orchard and what the different pricing schemes and potential profit margins will be this year.

He drops to the ground and examines some drying cover crop leaves. "They're full of mites," he announces.

A knot instantly forms in my stomach. Immediately I think of the damage mites can cause and what I could spray to control them. Old habits are hard to break.

"But I've never seen this species in a peach tree."

I relax, embarrassed by my reaction. I look through his lens, don't recognize the little spiderlike creatures, and am happy they would rather stay in the clover. We both walk out of the orchard with the knowledge that the peach crop will probably be fine. Should we become too confident, nature will put a stop to our foolishness. In the meantime, it's wonderful to feel satisfied without knowing or even caring exactly why.

## Five Worms

"Five worms."

I ask Pat to repeat.

"Five worms, I found five worms in your peaches." Pat has just finished one of his weekly data-gathering searches at my farm.

"What kind of worms?"

His voice is calm. "OFM. Oriental fruit moth."

That's not what I mean. I want to know the size of the worms, their color, and are they eating leaves or peaches? I ask, "Are the worms ugly?"

He pauses and I try to collect my thoughts. Then he says, "I'm not as familiar with OFM," and tries to comfort the shaken farmer by adding, "The peach twig borer populations are low, real low."

My eyes grow wide and I stare blankly out toward my fields. I mumble "Five worms" to myself.

I drive out to the field and Pat follows in his truck. The green peaches are growing fat, the size of Christmas decorations. The leaves flutter in a breeze like thousands of baby bird wings. Nervous anxiety builds and I start to search for worms, but I stop. I have no idea where to look.

Pat sits in his truck, procrastinating with a data log before joining me in the field. I plunge into a dozen questions. "What do OFM larvae look like at this time of year? They aren't after my green peaches yet, are they? Do other farmers have an outbreak?" I end with my most important one: "Pat, how many more worms are there?"

Pat shrugs. "I'm not sure. Like I said, OFM's not my thing. But I did do some reading." He launches into a ten-minute lecture on oriental fruit moth, and I learn more in those few minutes than in all my years on the farm. When five worms munch on your trees, your learning curve accelerates.

Initially I want to quantify the problem, break it down into dollars and cents.

Before, I used to apply a pesticide in winter that took care of all these worm problems. It wasn't expensive, maybe $20 per acre, for which I'd also get a low-stress spring and summer. But my natural-farming attempt is quickly becoming expensive for the nerves.

I ask, "Where did you find the five worms? Does each tree have five worms? Each branch?"

"Oh, no," Pat answers. "I looked at dozens of trees."

I relax a little. Five worms divided by two dozen trees means only a few worms per acre. But this could be the beginning of a new hatch, with only the first wave having emerged.

Pat explains how he found the worms. He inspects each branch for tiny half-inch or smaller worms or any visible signs of their feeding. It requires hours to inspect a dozen trees. "You've never found an OFM?" he asks.

"To tell you the truth, I've never looked," I blurt. "And I doubt if any farmer has ever committed an entire day to searching hundreds of branches for worms. No wonder you found some, looking so damned hard." I occurs to me that I may always have had five worms in my spring orchard and never knew it because no one spent hours obsessed with finding them. I ask again, "So how many worms do you think are out here?"

Pat shrugs again.

I'm not used to that kind of answer. Pesticide salesmen never shrug their shoulders. In fact they would love my situation: five worms, peach crop threatened, worried farmer, instant sales. Farmer paranoia and good sales commissions go hand in hand.

"What do five worms mean?" I mumble out loud. Pat smiles and says that sounds like a Zen master's question. I glare at him and he wanders over to another row of peaches.

The five worms challenge my attempt to farm these peaches differently. Their discovery threatens my organic methods, all the work I've tried this year. I sense a coming crisis of faith, knowing I could spray and kill all the worms in the field but then possibly repeat another ordinary harvest of homeless peaches. I have been hoping my alternative farming practices would become a marketing tool, leverage to get attention for these wonderful-tasting fruits.

But how can I live with nature? By learning to live with five worms and my stress? I realize that for the rest of the season, with the early morning rising sun or at nightfall with the heat lingering in the air, I'll stand on my farmhouse porch thinking about five worms.

I join Pat and we scan a few branches of leaves and green peaches. "Thanks for letting me know about the five worms," I say. He nods. "By the way, what did you do with them?" I grin. "I'd like to see their squashed bodies."

Pat turns to me with wide eyes and a blank look.

## Learning to Fail

The farm is never far away from my family. Our produce comes from the work of family. On the Masumoto farm our fruits and garden vegetables have been family food for generations.

My eight-year-old daughter, Nikiko, has witnessed both the successes and the failures of our farm. She has touched and tasted ripening fruits and has watched the power of weather unleashed on the fields. She knows her father is vulnerable to things out of his control. The farm is part of her picture drawing. She watches spring thunderstorms march into our valley and ravage tender green shoots with a downpour of hail. As the first ice balls crash down from the heavens, she sees me stand outside under the darkened sky and cry out, "Stop!" Later she draws a picture of the storm with a farmer wearing a big hat to protect himself.

We plant an annual vegetable garden, and this year Nikiko helps plant some of the seeds and seedlings. But after growing initially, they begin to die.

Nikiko's garden is failing. A virus attacks the fragile squash, causing the leaves to yellow and the delicate growth to wither. Her eggplants glisten from a sticky juice secreted by a herd of aphids with a company of tending ants. A phantom creature even munches on the hardy marigolds, taking huge circular bites out of the dangling leaves.

Daily I monitor the slow death, assessing the new damage, wondering if I should do something drastic. I consider using a garden spray, but when I read the label from the typical hardware store garden dust or pest spray, I realize it would be deadlier than anything I use on the farm. It will kill the aphids along with everything else, not the lesson I would want the garden to convey to my child. I face the same dilemma as I try to find a home for my Sun Crest peaches. If something doesn't work right I have to fight the tendency to find a quick solution.

"It's OK, Dad," Niki explains. "We have other squash plants." Then she quickly gives the napping dog a hug and skips over to the sunning cats for their afternoon tea together.

Nikiko helps me realize the difference between disappointment and losing. Her garden, like farming, teaches me that at times failure is OK.

I've lost raisin crops, peach harvests, whole trees and vines. I've lost money, time, and my labor. I've lost my temper, my patience, and, at times, hope. Most of the time, it's due to things beyond my control, like the weather, market prices, or insects or disease. Even in situations where I believe I am in charge— cover-crop seeding, management of workers, the timing of harvest—I now know I can never really have complete control.

Ironically, the moment I step off my farm I enter a world where it seems that everything, life and nature, is regulated and managed. Homes are built to insulate families from the outside weather. People work in climate-controlled environments designed to reduce the impact of the weather. The government develops bureaucracies and statutes to safeguard against failure and protect us from risk. In America, a lack of control implies failure.

As a kid I was taught that sports is a great training field for life, where you learn about the difference between winning and losing. But you also learn to make excuses to avoid looking like a failure. It's far easier to blame someone or something—a teammate who couldn't catch a fly ball, a lousy referee—than it is to learn to live with losses.

On the farm, the foul lines aren't marked and nature doesn't play by a rule book. There are no winners and losers and the game is never finished. There's always next year and the next harvest, more dark clouds on the horizon or aphids in your child's garden.

I also learned something about failure from my father. One year it began to rain on our raisin crop. A year's worth of work lay on the ground, exposed and vulnerable to the elements. The rain would soon begin to rot the harvest. I remember running outside to tell the clouds to go away. I came back inside and watched my father grow angry too. Restless, we walked back and forth to the window to check the march of dark clouds and listened to the *tap-tap-tap* of rain on the roof.

"What can we do?" I blurted out in frustration.

"What *can* you do?" he answered. "Make it stop raining?"

We lost most of the crop that year. We failed. But the grapes grew the next year and it didn't rain.

When I farm or garden, I learn to fail without winners or losers.

## *The* Furin

A small *furin* hangs on our farmhouse porch. Its miniature bell delicately jingles with the slightest breeze. A long strip of paper captures the air currents and translates the movement into sound. I can peer out over the fields, watching the advancing spring season with its green blankets of foliage, and hear the wind.

Nikiko likes the fragile sounds. The metal chime rings like a whisper, the voice tiny like a child's. Occasional spring winds in the valley blow strong enough to snap the outstretched vine canes. Most of the time soft breezes brush our cheeks with such subtleties that we ignore their presence. A *furin* reminds grown-ups what children already sense. Niki says she hears the wind singing.

I spend the spring battling nature, trying to farm differently, hoping somehow I am contributing to the quest to save my peach. The more I struggle, the more the burden seems to weigh. Each new approach generates more questions; the complexity of working with nature slips into a growing pattern of chaos.

I remember a Japanese saying about the power of bamboo. Its strength is not found in a rigid structure that blocks the wind; instead, the stalks bend with the wind. Their power resides in their very flexibility. I'm working on becoming like bamboo. I've abandoned my attempts to control and compete with nature, but letting go has been a challenge.

I'm trying to listen to my farm. Before, I had no reason to hear the sounds of nature. The sole strategy of conventional farming seems to be dominance. Now, with each passing week, I venture into fields full of life and change, clinging to a belief in my work and a hope that it's working.

As I recall the past spring from my porch, the ringing of the *furin* helps me understand as it flutters in a subtle breeze. For the first time in my life, I see the wind.

*summer harvest*

# summer work

## *Summer Dreams*

Summer hits with a blaze of heat, defying the calendar and my scheduling of farmwork. Some years it begins in early May, other years the first blast is delayed until mid-June. Temperatures rise to 100 degrees and I begin a routine of the two- or three-T-shirt workday. I sweat so much that by midmorning my shirt will be drenched, so I'll peel it off, leave it in the sun to dry, and pull on another. I repeat the ritual at noon, and by my afternoon work session I can recycle the dry morning shirt. Within minutes, though, I begin sweating. I can never predict the arrival of this first heat wave and instead find myself collapsed on the porch after foolishly trying to work straight through that first scorching day.

The burning heat lingers even as the sun settles on the horizon. The mud caked on my boots, now cured and dried, breaks off in small piles next to my outstretched legs. My damp shirt clings to my flesh, with an odd chill creeping across my back. My face rests on the wood boards, the knots smooth against my cheek. Between the planks I feel a kiss of cool air rising from the darkness below. I listen to our golden retriever, Jake, panting, releasing his body heat. I open my mouth too, trying to allow more heat to escape so I can recover from the annual initiation of summer.

My body knows a full day's work lies behind it. My legs and back ache from trudging through fields, my arms and hands are sore from working a shovel and from the irrigation water, even my worn boots pinch chafed heels and weary soles.

I catch myself dreaming of better weather, better harvests, better prices for my peaches—perhaps I will find a home for my wonderful-tasting produce. Then I scold myself for such fantasies and try to anticipate the inevitable disappointment. Dreams haunt farmers, they drive us through depression, disaster, and hunger and later tease our optimism with hope.

The greatest challenge of my summer remains: to keep the confidence I had when I turned back the bulldozer from my peach trees. If I lack vision of the coming harvest and lose my trust in nature, the year will be a constant struggle and perhaps futile. I'd best arm myself early in the season with righteous optimism.

With the first heat of summer and a glimpse of the coming season of work, dreams creep into my mind. I allow them to visit. For a moment, while resting on my porch, the sweat drying on my back, I feel content. Perhaps this is why we farmers continue: we work from moment to moment with the land, dreams fill us like a song or vision, and, for a brief pause, all is as it should be.

## Gourmet Dust

All good farmers become connoisseurs of dirt and dust. We have progressed from trailing a horse-drawn plow and marching through mud to riding modern equipment that elevates us three or four feet above the ground. But no good farmer can escape contact with the earth, we feel it on our tongues and in our throats.

Farm dust varies with soil types and regional cuisines. I don't know how the Georgia red clay tastes, but I have visited the Wisconsin dairy lands and Washington's Skagit Valley. Mixed with rains and lush growth, their dust is heavy and thick and has a richness, like a fattening dessert of chocolate.

Dust from the San Joaquin Valley of California contains subtle nuances of flavor only the native may detect. The denser clays of the northern valley have a smell of river history mingled within them. The Sacramento and San Joaquin rivers drain into this lowland area, depositing centuries of topsoil collected from a valley three hundred miles long. The dust from the western half of the valley is parched, baked. For centuries only sparse vegetation grew there until irrigation water was imported from northern California. Few rivers or streams cross the territory, and underground water tables are buried hundreds of feet deep. Winds blowing over the barren lands churn up storms of dust. The particles whip upward into visible clouds that drift to the east, lightly coating the farms of the eastern valley. In intense winds, I can see a dingy layer of air and sense what dust bowl veterans of the thirties must have witnessed.

My farm is on the east side of the valley, fed by rivers draining from the Sierras. I work land that was once part of an ancient lake that covered the entire valley. I now consider this land
a desert because our annual rainfall is often in the single digits.

My dust is a fine powder. The soil is a sandy loam that would
be a chef's delight. Add water to the earth and create a rich
roux, thick but pliable. Stir, and the air will be filled with a rich
aroma of turned earth. Beat the ground with a disk, and the
topsoil stands like sifted flour awaiting flavoring.

Without water, my ground is ripe for dust. In the heat of
summer a dust cloud follows all movement. Walking creates
delicate billows, tiny dirt particles take flight and dance around
my boots. I monitor Jake chasing a rabbit by the speeding column of dust suspended in his wake. A truck driving along the
field's edge becomes coated with a frosting of dirt.

I work my fields according to the dust. No dust suggests that
the soil is too wet; tractor tires will compact the ground and
crush the dirt particles together, causing farm equipment to scar
the land with cementlike impressions. Erratic puffs of dust suggest that the ground is too dry, the earth baked so hard that little
can break through the crust. Disks and cultivators bounce over
the parched surface, pulverizing the thin topsoil without penetrating the root zones. A battered and abused layer of dirt is left
behind, bared to winds that scatter particles high into the air.

The dust layers on my eyelashes. Blinking creates miniature
clouds before my eyes. Even my unexposed skin wears a fine
undergarment of dust; it penetrates most every crevice of my
body. I've found dust in places I could only see in a mirror.
When body moisture mixes with this dust, little streaks appear
on my skin and my clothes. The combination generates an uncomfortable friction.

I lick my lips often when working in the dust. It has a delicate flavor, quiet yet seasoned with a certain tanginess. Growing

juicy peaches and grapes amid these conditions seems like a
contradiction, yet the dust tempers the character of my fruits.
My Sun Crest peaches are sweet but not like candy. My grapes
have a delicate taste, light and almost surprising. They both perform well in my soils. My land is balanced, and her dust com-
plements my labor the way a subtle dry wine adds to a meal.

## Summer Pruning

I know a secret about pruning: it begins in the summer. Years
ago I first read about summer pruning in a university research
report that examined, in detail, "fruitwood budding physiology
during the critical summer growth." From the author I concluded that good fruitwood—wood that will have a wealth of
blossoms by the next spring and strong stems that can bear lots
of large, fat peaches—is formed during the summer. But I discovered it would take years to transfer the research from the
paper to the field.

Farmers call those branches where peaches dangle hangers, I
suppose, either because fruit hangs on them or the slender stems
hang down from the main limbs. Contrary to common percep-
tion, though, a well-pruned fruit tree does not have all its
branches pointing upward. A skinny branch, reaching for the
heavens, would probably snap under the weight of two or three
midsummer peaches, swollen with juice—a painful sight for
the anxious farmer.

During the summer I'm not much concerned about hangers.
I'm more concerned about the overall shape of the tree. A properly trained fruit tree resembles a goblet, its major limbs trained
upward from the trunk, not too straight up like a champagne
glass but rather angled outward with the gentle curve of a wine-
glass. If a tree adopts the shape of a martini glass, however, it

will have a poor structural character, and with a heavy crop the main scaffolds will break. It helps to know your adult beverages when you prune.

Dad once had a nectarine orchard where, over the years, we let all the growth migrate upward. At eye level and below, few branches ever survived because the treetops blocked much of the sunlight. Walking under the lush growth, I felt as if I had entered a natural cathedral, with arches suspended ten to fifteen feet above and hallow earth below. This may have been great for a pious experience but it was lousy for the business of farming, because pruning, fruit thinning, and harvesting had to be done mostly from ladders, with workers precariously perched twelve feet in the air. It was expensive and time-consuming, and it tested one's sense of balance. Each year it only got worse, the top growth reaching higher and higher, competing for sunlight.

To combat such vigorous growth, some farmers bring in a wicked-looking machine called a tree topper. It resembles a mechanical spider with saw-blade arms, something you might see in a cheap horror movie about science gone amok. This machine has four giant circular saws, mounted horizontally on revolving arms that rise above the canopy, which slice and dice and chop everything from about ten feet up. It's a robotic tree barber, attacking an orchard and giving it a flattop. The sound of the buzzing saws and shattering wood terrorizes; what's left behind is a field of slashed and severed limbs.

For a few weeks following the tree clipping, warm sunlight penetrates the trees and they respond with wonderful growth. But a study done by University of California researchers verifies what some farmers have witnessed: cutting a limb at the peak growing season only stimulates new shoots just below the incision. New growth pushes upward even thicker and the flattop soon grows back denser than ever, with two or three new shoots reaching for sunlight where only one stood before. You can't manipulate nature for too long.

A healthy tree will sprout unwanted suckers and water spouts. These lush fast-growing shoots grow from the center of the tree, wasting plant energy and nutrients. Eventually they begin to shade out and kill the lower branches. Pruning them in summer can only help the tree.

I had had no prior experience with summer pruning; most farmers omit the practice. It may have to do with the time— summer is full of other work demands and farmers have to run in order to keep up with the heat of harvest. On the other hand, maybe we just think of pruning as a foggy-weather task. This methodical off-season chore feels odd in the sweltering heat.

Then I discovered why I was one of the few who summer-pruned. In 100-degree heat, when you cut too much growth and expose branches to direct sunlight, the bark roasts and burns. The wood blisters and then cracks, exposing the delicate inter-nal cork layers to insects and disease. Wood borers love wounded limbs and quickly move in and make themselves at home. In one of my orchards most of the trees have lost their east limbs, casualties of my first attempt at summer pruning.

After trial and error, I learned that I can trim my trees in summer, but pruning is the wrong word for it. It should be called summer shaping. I can shape a tree in summer and not only encourage growth near the ground but become a bonsai artist, a sculptor gently guiding a healthy shoot into an open area to fill in space where a branch has died. Done properly, each tree becomes uniquely balanced in a natural symmetry.

Trees don't let you forget your mistakes, especially pruning. Badly pruned trees stay with a farmer for years. I have some trees that will never be properly shaped, and every time I pass them I'm reminded of my mistakes of years before.

I read of a Japanese wood craftsman who spoke about free-ing the soul of a tree. Like a sculptor, I too labor to free that soul. But the souls of my trees and vines are alive and they respond to my actions. I live with them daily.

## Fixing Leaks

At first, I try to ignore the brown, muddy stain in the middle of the dirt avenue. But the next day a miniature spring with a pool of water sits in the roadway: my irrigation pipeline is leaking.

Like all orchards and vineyards in this area, my Sun Crest orchards use an irrigation system that carries water to the thirsty trees and vines. With water, the valley flourishes from a desert into a garden.

Most of the smaller open ditches of yesterday have been re-placed by concrete irrigation pipelines. They run like a maze underground, connecting fields to a pump or other water source. I don't know when some of my lines were laid. A ten-incher is pre–World War II vintage, when most farms had small pumps, small fields, and perhaps lower expectations. In the seventies, Dad added a 15-horsepower deep-well pump that requires a fourteen-inch line to feed his quarter-mile-long vine rows. Other lines lie hidden still and have yet to be identified. I don't know how deep a particular line may be buried, or what quirks would have led a farmer to substitute an odd-sized sec-tion when he ran out of standard cement pipe, or where the line curves because the land was inaccurately surveyed and that's where the property line was originally drawn. I could not antic-ipate these idiosyncrasies of my farm.

I drive closer to inspect the newly formed pool of water in the avenue. The leak grows with each day, the continual water pressure in the line forcing the crack to expand. I hope it will somehow heal itself like a small wound (sometimes fine sand particles can lodge in small cracks and slow the seepage). By the third day, however, I can no longer drive over the expanding puddle without the risk of getting stuck. The time to repair the crack has arrived.

I begin the job by digging a hole but soon discover that I have to know how deep I must go. For pacing, I need to envision my target or I risk the wrong rhythm. I may start too quickly and exhaust my back and arms, which will inevitably lead to a bad attitude. Or I may proceed too slowly, which, with the sun beating down upon me, will drain my energy and spirit.

When I fix a leak, I master some very basic engineering skills: the deeper the hole, the wider it needs to be, not for structural support or safety but for fit. A hole five feet deep requires a working space at least four feet across. I need to have enough room to straddle the pipe and punch a hole in the concrete. I must have space to crouch over and reach into the line to coat the crack with cement.

Most of my irrigation lines run between three and five feet below the surface and require a rather large hole. The holes also seem deeper because, as I remove earth, a pile of dirt grows around me, proportionate with the hole. A four-by-four-foot hole five feet deep contains a huge amount of dirt. The mounds make me think of hunkering down for trench warfare.

Fixing a leak becomes a war of contradictory forces. Cracks often form at the weakest point where the pressure is the greatest—in other words, where the line is the deepest. Also consider the fact that wet earth weighs more than dry. The deeper I dig, burrowing closer to the leak, the more mud I excavate. Finally, the concrete pipe needs to be dry in order for a cement patch to bond and seal, but these lines are filled with water. So I have to pump all the water out before patching.

I use an old gas-powered pump, the motor permanently borrowed from a discarded lawn mower. Starting the motor is a
challenge. Swearing rarely helps, though pleading seems to
have an effect as I delicately adjust the balance between the
choke and the fuel mixture and the proper tug on the cord.
After the hundredth pull, and quick reflexes to tap the choke
partially inward, I triumph: a puff of exhaust is released, a sput-
tering begins, and *voilà!* the engine finally starts.

But that's just the first test. I still need to prime the pump.
The source of the water sits five to six feet below ground level.
Water has to be drawn upward and pushed out with a strong
suction. After I punch a hole in the pipe large enough to slip in a
hose, I try to siphon water in and air out by rapidly lifting and
dropping the hose, shaking out air pockets and hoping water
will snake in. An hour later, feet numb from standing in mud, I
manage to coax out enough air and a prime is established; water
gushes out and into my fields. Since the leak often occurs at the
lowest portion of the pipe, water flows into the section from
everywhere on the farm. It may require hours to drain the line.
I keep vigil so that I don't lose my prime and the pump doesn't
run out of gas.

Once a neighbor hired an irrigation company to come out
and fix some leaks. They worked hard and did the job well, but
for six hours they sat, waiting for the pump to drain the line.
They ate lunch, took a nap, read part of a newspaper, walked
around on the farm, and drove into town for coffee. Just when
they left for town their pump ran out of gas. As soon as they returned they refilled the small tank and resumed their waiting.
Those six hours just about killed my neighbor. He'd come by
and check on their progress and calculate the cost of their water
watch and instantly become a prime candidate for a heart attack. Farmers work at a different pace. They don't sit around
and wait.

Cement is the farmer's clay. With a proper blend of cement, sand, and water, rolled into a pliable ball and then gently molded along the seam, masterpieces are created inside cracked pipelines. A smooth patch is a work of art, the laborer a craftsman. Like the artist who works not for an audience but for the sake of art, we seal our work within the pipe.

I feel more like an apprentice, since most of my time is spent setting up in order to patch the leak. I trench and excavate a huge hole, locate the leak and punch an access slot, then sit and monitor the draining water. Reaching into the pipe preparing the surface for the wet cement, I'll scrape my arms and rub my knuckles raw. My legs will ache from the preparation work, cramped quarters, and odd angles as I straddle the line.

The consistency of my cement and sand mixture is never the same and I lack the confidence to trust a thin, gentle coat along a seam. My patches become gobs of cement, a bucket of concrete slapped together in wads resembling a protruding blood vessel. The hole resembles a battleground, with cement dripping from the pipe and splattered along the earthen walls, not to mention some of my own blood from scrapes and cuts. I am positive I will acquire trench foot from the hours of standing in water. I do not yet consider myself an artist.

But like a true apprentice, my work improves with each job and progress is duly noted as the next irrigation round begins. I check the spots I've worked and discover that the earth remains dry.

I don't know of many farmers who think of themselves as cement artists, and few artists consider blue-collar hand laborers their peers. But some farmers and artists share a common understanding that their work is often incomplete, their craft still developing. As the summer unfolds and my strategies to save my peaches take shape, I realize that few problems are ever solved. A farmer fixes leaks in pipelines, an artist progresses to the next challenge, and I know that come the time for a future irrigation, I'll find more leaks.

## Babies and Mildew

I have a confession. I plan to use a chemical on some of my grapes to kill mildew (although I'll keep a small block un-sprayed and organic). I have struggled with the dilemma for days. This contradicts my belief in natural farming practices, al-though the chemical won't harm humans. But I've thought it out and I think it's worth it to spray to lessen my tedious work-load so I can spend more time with my family.

Mildew hides all spring and summer. The spores overwinter in my field, grow in the cool days of spring, and thrive in the mi-croclimates of lush grape-leaf canopies. You can't see them re-producing and spreading. Untreated, mildew coats young grape berries with spores that will quickly infect and strangle tissue. With the summer heat, the tiny berries swell but their skin has grown brittle. The flesh cracks and juices ooze out and coat the entire bunch. They will drip onto neighboring bunches and rot will invade. Then insects arrive, feeding and breeding on the rotting meat.

Because this enemy is invisible during the early stages of growth, I can't walk my fields to check for damage, I don't see chewing creatures munching on my crop, and I can't check to see if my control methods are working. So I must treat preven-tively, usually with a series of dustings of sulfur, a few pounds an acre every seven days for two to three months. Should a spring shower wash the fields, I must reenter as soon as the fields dry and recoat the bunches with more sulfur, which sucks the moisture out, drying any environment conducive to mildew.

Farmers have used sulfur for generations; it has in fact been effective for centuries. Some people are allergic to it—my eyes burn when I'm dusting, and if the wind gusts in the wrong direction, my skin will smell of sulfur for days. The treatment program remains simple and it works. Sulfur doesn't kill per se. Instead, it wreaks havoc on mildew's habitat, destroying the damp interiors of grape bunches and dense leaf clusters. For that reason, mildew strains haven't built up resistance, like other pests, and sulfur doesn't appear to be very toxic to other life. But you have to keep on schedule, every week without fail, without interruption. That can leave little time for family.

I talk with a pest control adviser, a bug man who helps monitor fields and gives farmers recommendations on controlling problems.

"Is something wrong with your sulfur program?" he asks.

"No, nothing's wrong." I know I sound defensive. "But I'm looking for an alternative to sulfuring all the time."

My adviser then develops a three-year plan with lots of scheduled purchases and sales commissions. When I try to explain why I am looking for an alternative in the first place, he can't understand my paradox. "Don't think so much," he cautions.

Ironically his advice helps. My decision is narrowed when Nikiko asks, "Daddy, why do you always smell like sulfur?"

I decide to use a systemic fungicide on my grapes, which, according to the advertising, "provides weeks of residual control." I will only have to spray once a month. The poison will attack my mildew, destroy it, and keep the grapes clean for weeks. I will enjoy the free evenings to spend with my family, and when we hug they'll smell my flesh.

But I hope no one drops by and sees the bags of fungicides. I imagine a skeptical neighbor stopping in, grinning as I dump the toxic powder into my sprayer, nodding his head in an I-told-you-so fashion. Later he may call me a hypocrite or remark that

I've regained my senses. I guiltily imagine a stranger judging my work, ignoring my green cover crops with their ladybugs and lacewings, never acknowledging that I've changed my farming practices to safer, less destructive pest controls. All the stranger will see and remember is my last decision: I'm the farmer who uses a poison on his grapes.

I am reminded that in some valley wells they have found traces of a chemical called DBCP (dibromochloropropane) in ground water aquifers. DBCP was linked to sterility in males and is now banned in the United States. My dad used some DBCP years ago. It was supposed to kill nematodes, microscopic pests that chewed up roots. No one knew it would contaminate drinking water. Neighboring city folks are angry with farmers for damaging their water supply. "How could you farmers poison the water?" they ask.

My dad didn't choose to pollute the water table. He did nothing illegal. He simply trusted the chemical company and the governmental regulatory agencies. He made a decision based on a recommendation from a pest control consultant, advice that turned out to be bad. Dad acknowledges his mistake and asks, "What do you want me to do now?"

Yet I still hear angry people who blame the farmers. "Those farmers used the poison, didn't they? It was their choice, wasn't it?" Newspapers write headlines: FARMERS CONTAMINATE THE ENVIRONMENT. Farmers are portrayed as polluters. People remember your last decision as your only decision. My dad grows embittered. Suddenly I feel even more torn about my decision to spray.

# a family farm

## Family Dinner Tables

I work a family farm. My parents, wife, and children spend time in the fields. They help with chores and give advice and suggestions. Their presence inspires and motivates. My extended family also influences the way I farm, either through conversations, comments, and occasional criticism or through my memories of growing up with uncles, aunts, and cousins on the farm. They are part of the historical landscape that defines my family farm. Even Marcy's family plays a role.

Marcy's extended family has been farming for generations in the rich Wisconsin dairy land region. I've discovered an odd affinity with her family and their farm communities. They're German Catholic and Lutherans instead of Japanese American Christians and Buddhists. They have dairies and cows and grow corn, while we in California have peaches and grapes and make raisins. But we both share a strong sense of family, something that is keenly displayed at the dinner table.

Marcy's Grandma Rose reminds me of my *baachan*. Both surviving farm matriarchs have outlived their spouses by decades, continue to value hard work, and remain deeply spiritual and physically strong. They consider family meals a centerpiece to farm life, though their approaches differ greatly.

Grandma Rose comes to life in the planning and serving of family dinners. She considers homegrown produce superior to anything store-bought. A neighbor's gift of garden peas is welcomed at meals, and bartered goods—beans for a granddaughter's baby sitting services—achieve special homegrown status. She values knowing where foods come from and who is responsible for them; she honors them by attaching names to dishes. Around the dinner table I can hear, "Please pass Glady's squash" or "Little John's first deer venison sausage." Even my California raisins have a place at the table; after Marcy and I were married, she called them "Mas's raisins."

Food often becomes the focus of mealtime conversations. Grandma Rose's history unfolds as we talk of apple orchards, summer fruit canning, and summer sausage. She educates me about root cellars that housed a winter's menu of sausages hanging from racks to piles of produce preserved for months by Wisconsin's hard, deep snows. Even bratwurst contains a flavor of history. When I eat a meal of "brats and kraut," I not only learn who grew the cabbage and made the sauerkraut but also am apprised of the evolution of the "brat"—where the pig was raised, who butchered the animal (and if an agreement was made for the butcher to keep a full ham), and who stuffed the links with their secret blend of spices. Fortunately she refrains from announcing the name of the creature that gave its life for our meal. Instead the family tries to decipher the secret of the spice blend.

(In order to continue the bratwurst tradition, Marcy once had an office party to celebrate a California-style Oktoberfest. She made a door sign inviting everyone to our farm that read BYOBB: BRING YOUR OWN BEER AND BRATS. Some of our guests apparently didn't get it. One of them couldn't figure out why she was the only one who brought kids to the party!)

I can understand why Grandma Rose's family consumed lots of meat and potatoes. Fresh produce was a luxury, arriving only in summer. Yet traditions take time to change, and despite the fact that fresh produce is now available year round, she still plans meals featuring lots of meat and only an occasional stewed fruit or overcooked vegetable. Once during a visit, I devoured a lettuce leaf garnish, longing for something fresh. I realized that a regional cuisine is firmly entrenched in these farm communities.

Family traditions accompany meals. In Wisconsin, going to Grandma's house for Sunday dinner means a visit to the farm. The sons and daughters are obligated to return home, and the adult kids still slip to their designated spots around the family dinner table. Grandma Rose insists that the family wait until everyone has arrived before starting dinner. Grandchildren complain and adults comment about the perpetually late brother, but the family will wait and then begin the meal with a prayer.

For Grandma Rose, grace before a meal represents an affirmation of family strength. I can hear her commanding voice, with family gathered before her: "Blessed art thou . . . " She speaks loudly as if, by example, she will encourage everyone to join in. The family follows Grandma Rose's lead; then halfway through her voice grows soft. I wonder if she's checking to make sure everyone is participating in their daily rite of gratitude to the Lord.

Occasionally I sneak a peek and can see her gazing at the family with her glassy eyes. At first it appears she's conducting a head count, but her eyes move too slowly as she pans the bowed heads and faces of her family. During our last visit with her I thought I saw her old, tired eyes begin to water and tear with the delivery of grace.

I WOULD LIKE to say that Baachan also speaks to us through her cooking, but that is not true. The Masumoto clan comes from peasant stock, we are not samurai. We know more about growing, harvesting, and carrying buckets of produce than we know about preparing fine meals.

The legacy of Baachan's cooking remains. We serve rice at most meals. She often made *okazu,* her term for anything stir fried and served with white rice, or *gohan*. She would add meat or fish if it was available. In her later years, "washing the rice" was her contribution to meals. She would rinse and drain uncooked rice (originally to remove dirt and talc) and set it aside to soak for hours before cooking.

Taking responsibility for the rice also served as Baachan's method of assembling the family. I remember that when I was a teenager, she'd survey every family member to ask who would be at dinner. Her excuse was that she needed to determine how much rice to wash; I believe it was really her strategy for gathering the family for a meal.

Sometimes she'd walk out into the fields and flail her arms, waving to get my attention. When I'd see her, panic would run through my thoughts. "What happened? Was there an accident at home?"

But she would simply ask, "*Gohan?*"

I would nod and commit to stay at home for family dinner. She would trot home, her mission completed: a teenage grandson taken care of for another evening.

I most vividly remember Baachan carrying buckets of vegetables or fruit from the fields into the kitchen for meal preparation. She'd balance two buckets, one in each hand, both filled so full that the top layers had to be individually stacked in a pyramid design, each fruit strategically placed to hold the one above it. As she trudged along the dirt path, I could see her dust shadow trailing behind her. She would drag her feet slightly in order to glide across the uneven terrain. The buckets pulled her arms, whose blood vessels protruded from the weight; the wire handle must have felt like a knife cutting into her palms. I could see her knuckles turn white. Yet she journeyed on, intent on delivering her contribution.

During meals, Baachan would remain quiet, sitting in a corner rather than at the head of the table. As soon as we were done, she'd pounce on the dirty dishes and start putting away leftovers. Wasting food was not tolerated. She didn't *say* much about a wasted plateful of food, but by piling it on a single tray for our dogs and letting it sit for all to see, she communicated clearly.

Despite being born and raised on opposite sides of the earth, both grandmothers share a common history of poverty that made simply getting food on the table a challenge. They must shake their heads at today's change in attitudes—being wasteful, especially with food, remains a sin for them. Not only is food part of their livelihood, it carries a special significance: a communion with family.

I wonder if my peaches belong to a past generation, those who savor produce and value the taste of natural foods. Sun Crests are not to be consumed like fast food. I agree with my grandmothers when they call my peaches "family food."

## Knowing Your Father's Work

I return to my daily field walks and watch the peaches and grapes grow fat. Perhaps only a farmer would find it exciting to begin talking to himself in conversations filled with farmer jargon. "The fruit needs to put on size." "They're just beginnin' to break color." "I can see the first blush with just a hint of jet green."

The cover crops and weeds mingle in the fields. In some places the clover dominates and grows like a green carpet, in others the weeds have taken over and choke the earth with their thick stalks. I wonder how much they compete for water, nutrients, and root space.

Sometimes the family takes an evening walk or bike ride with me, but I make a poor companion unless the topic centers on the farm, on peaches or water or weather. I can't help but stop and pull a weed as we walk, making a mental note about a broken vineyard wire or noticing a sagging tree limb I will need to prop. Sometimes I jam a stick in the dirt along our path as a reminder, flagging the spot for work tomorrow.

Even if I try to concentrate on a conversation about Marcy's work or Nikiko's school or two-year-old Korio's entry into a new childhood phase, my metaphors revolve around the farm. I try to compare Marcy's work with farming, but vines and trees do not behave like her staff or hospital management team members, although sometimes my pest control strategies would seem more appropriate for her challenges. Niki's daily school lessons are more like mine. We both share a hunger for discovery and new knowledge, but also wish to have our daily seminars remain fun. As for Kori, he easily behaves like my young trees or vines, which need freedom to grow and explore under gentle guidance and training. As I walk the farm, I am unable to separate my work from my family.

I grew up knowing my father's work. He left in the early morning for places I often visited. Rarely did he return late, in darkness or at night, or weary with problems I could not imagine. I saw him at work daily and sometimes worked with him. As a young child I knew some of the crises he faced. I cringed at the sight of worms attacking ripe peaches. I too could feel the searing heat of the summer sun as it blistered exposed fruit. I would shiver with a late spring frost and watch the delicate fresh vine shoots turn brown and then black within hours from the freeze.

My children will know the work of their father too. But I show more emotions than my father did. My daughter has seen me yell at the approaching clouds of a September rain on my raisins and curse about lousy fruit prices when no one wants my peaches. My children know the thrill of driving a tractor: the roar of the diesel engine and the bouncing ride down dirt avenues with a tepid breeze stroking our faces. They are learning the skills of howling at a full moon in summer and sticking their heads out a pickup window, dodging gnats and bugs before they lodge in their mouths and throats. Our family is bound to the land. Our farm survives as both a home and a workplace.

When I was in college, I often enjoyed asking friends about their parents' work. I was interested in why people chose their professions and what their work meant to them. I thought my questions would become a safe method to get to know someone. But most of my friends never ventured beyond one-line answers: "My dad is an engineer" or "He works for a bank" or "He handles sheet metal for an air-conditioning company."

I'd respond, "What kind of engineer?" or "Why'd he choose banking?" or "How's the sheet-metal business?" Such questions alienated lots of friends. Family seemed to be a painful subject.

After I told them my dad was a farmer, rarely did they ask a second question. I stopped interpreting their initial response, "Oh, really?" as one of positive surprise. I realized the rise in their voice meant they had nothing else to say and had no intention of finding out more.

Following college and my return home, I felt uncomfortable telling others, "I farm." I translated blank looks as disdain mixed with condescension. I could see images flash through their minds of Old MacDonald and hayseeds who spend weekends watching corn grow. As my peers were securing their corporate jobs and advancing as professionals in law or medicine, I spent long lunch hours talking with my dad, getting to know fifty acres of vines and twenty acres of peach trees. I didn't know it at the time, but I was laying the groundwork to save the Sun Crest peaches.

It required hours of listening before I noticed that Dad's stories about his father, my *jiichan,* seemed to revolve around the pronoun "they" much more than "he." "They" meant Jiichan and Baachan or the entire family of four sons and two daughters. I had to adjust my thinking. My image of work was singular in nature, one man in one job, not of a family and their combined effort to make a living. I learned the significance of work that is inseparable from home, when work is also the place you live and play and sleep.

Dad tells the story of hot summer nights and Jiichan's wooden platform. Fresno's 100-degree days would beat down on the place where they lived, a shack with a tin roof that required hours to cool after sunset. They didn't have a cooler or fan—out in the country there was no electricity—but it didn't matter.

Jiichan made a low wooden platform from old barn wood. It rose about two feet off the ground with a top area big enough for all six kids. In the evenings, Jiichan led everyone outside and the whole family would lie on the platform, side by side, almost touching.

After a long day in the fields where they worked together as a family, and following a simple dinner and refreshing *ofuro,* a Japanese bath, the family gathered and began an evening ritual of talking, resting, and gazing upward at the night sky. The dirt yard was beneath them, the vineyards beginning a few feet away. If a little breeze came they could hear the grape leaves shifting and rustling, creating an illusion of coolness. It seemed to make everyone feel better.

Every summer the family lay outside into the late evening, until their shack home had cooled and they could go inside to sleep. Sometimes the boys would sleep all night on the platform, quiet and peaceful.

I too can remember sharing the dark sky of hot summer nights with my brother. We sometimes camped out in the fields. During a break between the summer fruits and the family packing-shed work, we pitched a homemade tent made from an old bedsheet and a tree rope. You would think working all summer with these peaches and grapes, we'd be weary of them, let alone want to sleep among them. But we wanted to sleep "in the wilderness" and drew no lines between our fields of play and the fields of work. This wasn't just any farm, it was our home.

We'd spend a night outdoors and witness the midsummer show of shooting stars. We'd play a game of spying the first meteor and then racing to point to the next and the next. We divided the heavens into sections, guessing whose would have the most meteors and how many we could see at the same time.

Just before we fell asleep I would hear Dad open the back door. I think he'd purposely let the door slam shut so we'd know of his presence. He'd stand listening to the sound of his fields with his sons sleeping out in the darkness. I knew he could smell us. In the windless summer nights, the smoke from our camp-fire would drift toward the house, a beacon revealing our loca-tion. After a few minutes I would hear the door slam shut again. He'd go to bed knowing all was well.

When I tell these stories to friends, their eyes widen and smiles come to their faces. They tell me how fine it must be to raise children on a farm. I now realize that the silence I experi-enced in college arose from a youthful notion that we could get away from our families. We were hoping to journey beyond the horizon, ignorant that what some of us actually sought was right in front of us.

I now know that saving my peach will involve more than competing with nature. It will necessarily include family as I create something called home.

## Home Pack

I can no longer delay the hunt, I force myself to stop walking the fields and embark on finding a market for these wonderful-tasting but homeless peaches. Too easily I've procrastinated with the excuse, "I grow the fruit, that's what I do best. Let someone else worry about selling it." I hope a miracle will hap-pen, a produce retailer reading the *L.A. Times* article about my peaches will become obsessed with my fruit. I base my fantasy on the thought that good things happen to good peaches. Marcy claims I am becoming a real farmer, "hopelessly naive."

I read a fruit marketing report that concludes that the major-ity of peach buyers either have children or are fifty-five years or older. This reinforces my belief in peaches as family food. My

Sun Crest peaches are the ideal fruit for both a mature generation and for children.

I pitch my "family food, not fast food" slogan to a few fruit brokers. These middlemen (and most of them are men) supposedly do all us farmers a favor by using their professional skills to find the best buyers for our fruits, creating a perfect match. On paper the system sounds fair, but in reality the buyer most always has the upper hand, especially with a perishable crop. Few deals are negotiated in advance. Instead, frantic brokers search for buyers as soon as the peaches are picked and packed in boxes, thousands of packages waiting shipment in cold storage.

"It's a stacked deck," one farmer explains. "There's a reason why we call them brokers. They're good at helping us farmers go broke."

I start with a series of phone calls, and over half the brokers laugh when I mention Sun Crest.

I ask, "Why the chuckle?"

They refer to a mysterious blacklist with Sun Crest near the top, tainted with a reputation for lousy color and terrible shelf life. Fruit brokers want peaches that last for weeks in cold storage without becoming mealy and soft. "We want color and shelf life, shelf life and color," I hear over and over. Sun Crests are stereotyped, condemned by a deeply entrenched prejudice. It would take a sixties-style revolution to overcome the bigotry.

"But the taste," I plead.

That brings even louder laughter from some.

I sense some hope when a few brokers ask, "What other varieties do you have?"

After a few calls, I learn more about the broker mentality, their high-stress jobs, and their appetite for humor. I learn to start conversations with my best joke (often about lawyers or sex), followed by name dropping (everyone seems to know one another). Eventually, conversation leads to a discussion of peaches. I first talk about my newer varieties, Elegant Ladies and Spring Ladies, then I nimbly slip in Sun Crest with a quick mumble.

I discern a positive breakthrough when one broker doesn't laugh and only asks, "How long do you plan to keep the Sun Crest?" A high school friend who is the salesman at a nearby packing house agrees to take my Sun Crest crop, providing I give their house the rest of my peaches. He understands some of my feelings about this peach and patronizes me. "We'll work with you and try our best," he assures me, then adds, "And if our price is less than it costs you to pick and pack them, we'll let you know before you throw good money after bad."

Not pick the crop? That is not one of my options. I think of becoming a broker myself, to find a home for at least some of my peaches. I could honestly say to buyers I know these peaches and have tasted their flavor. I could describe what's actually there: "Spring Lady peaches are sweet yet with the tangy flavor of early season fruit," or "Elegant Lady peaches are rich with flavor because I hang them on the tree a few days longer," and, of course, "Sun Crest has a buttery flavor that melts in your mouth, smooth and sweet with the message of summer in each bite." Perhaps my realism would be refreshing, especially if I got beyond the buyers to the actual retail produce people and consumers.

I talk with a few local produce managers about my peaches, and most agree to take some. But how will I deliver them, with my own truck? Suddenly I picture myself in the wholesale produce business instead of farming.

Some of my farmer friends tell me of their success in the farmer's market circuit. Many cities are reestablishing open-air markets: a downtown street closes for a morning, farmers back up their pickups and trucks and sell fresh local produce to eager shoppers hungry for good quality. The atmosphere is festive, the downtown is revitalized, and farmers make good money, providing their operation matches the weekly routine. But my farm is a long drive from the major urban markets in the Bay Area or in southern California, and instead of ten or twenty different peach varieties, with a staggered ripening time, my Sun Crests come all at once.

Still, I try to devise a farmer's market business plan. I envision Marcy quitting her job to work the San Francisco market, I'd handle southern California, and we'd each take one child to hand out peach samples. I imagine that once we total the travel expenses and the long hours we will not even make minimum wage, and our kids could turn us in for violating child labor laws.

Another option is to pick and pack some of the peaches myself. Perhaps I could harvest a specialty pack, an exclusive box with the best fruit commanding a higher price. By home packing I can sell a few hundred boxes, dealing directly with retailers and maybe covering enough production expenses to justify keeping the Sun Crests.

With the thought of home packing, a flood of memories rushes through my mind, a childhood of summers spent packing our own fruit. For kids growing up on a farm, summers were filled with family working together. It wasn't until I was about ten years old that I discovered that city families took summer vacations and kids got bored with nothing to do. I wasn't sure if I was lucky to have my summers filled with activity or cheated out of a vacation and a child's lazy summer memories. For us, summer meant work.

Our family was not unique. Much of the tree fruit industry of California began in a similar fashion. Before World War II, small family operations were the norm. In what was called "shade-tree packing," farmers parked a wagon under a large tree and packed their fruits into boxes destined for the nation. Some gradually expanded and moved into a barn, adding more equipment—a set of rollers and packing stands or later conveyor and sizing belts—and eventually developed today's sophisticated operation, which uses electronic-video-sensing sorting and computer-controlled belts and printouts. The industry matured with a great deal of cooperation, farmers banding together for marketing and quality control. The tree fruit community has remained a diverse collection of thousands of growers supplying a nation with summer fruits. We are still a community bound with a common history of home packing operations dependent on the hard work of family and neighbors.

I PLAN TO keep my specialty harvest very small, a throwback to the shade-tree era of farming. But first I need to round up the old fruit packing equipment to re-create the family operation.

I talk with Dad and plant the idea. I can see him searching his memory, wondering where he stored a certain roller or lidding stand. For the next few days I monitor his steady supply caravan as he drives the quarter mile from his place to mine, his latest discoveries hanging out the back of his pickup. He unloads them in my shed and returns home for more rediscovered treasures.

He locates pieces of equipment we haven't seen for years: a twelve-foot roller with a ninety-degree turn extension unit, a collection of ink stamps with fruit variety names, a wooden stand that held three boxes on top with lower shelves for packaging pads. Dad unveils a prize collection of picking buckets spanning the eras—from a wooden pail with metal bands (which I label FROM THE FRUIT STONE AGE), to the steel model that had a "reshaping" capability should a teenage farm boy run over it with a tractor (I recognize the place where I pounded out the dent with a hammer) and the most recent nineties all-plastic version.

I celebrate Dad's finds with long talks about the old days of home packing. Once we finish a conversation with a walk-through of the future packing shed, and Dad drags a stick in the dirt to draw outlines of where equipment can be set up.

My peaches will journey through a series of work stations, beginning with a type of brush-cleaner machine (which I still have to find or make), then onto a sorting table for packing. Sometimes the peaches will go directly from bucket into box, if they are not too fragile and if the buyer doesn't mind a little fuzz. The fruit will be packed into wooden boxes and pushed toward a lidding stand. A cover is then nailed on and the boxes stacked on a pallet, ready for shipment. Over the years, in the larger packing houses, new technology has been introduced: a washer and hydrocooler are used before the fruit is packed, along with conveyor belts with automated sizers, and card-board boxes, and hot-glue-gun sealers. But for our home packing operation, the people matter the most.

I remember the division of labor among family members, the women doing almost all the sorting and packing, the men bringing the fruit in and taking the filled boxes for lidding and palletizing. Each kid had a job. My older brother started lidding the boxes as soon as he could swing a hammer. Later, when I became of lidding age, my brother advanced up our corporate ladder and was promoted to truck loader. My sister packed fruit at the work station behind my mom. I remember Mom often turning around and checking on her daughter's box, monitoring for odd sizes or shapes of fruit and inspecting overall appearance. Even when my sister grew proficient and could pack better than anyone else in the shed, she remained at the number-two packing stand, part of a hierarchy that was entrenched in the family operation. I did lots of the little jobs, stamping and padding the boxes for the packers, assisting my brother when his roller got too full, tossing culls when they over-flowed their boxes and needed dumping. Everyone worked as a family team, even cousins, who came to work and stayed with us every summer. At the age of ten I started supervising my cousin.

We worked during the day, but having a live-in cousin as a best friend meant long hours of summer play after work. Every evening we'd have an instant family gathering, with ten kids running and playing games through the long sunlit hours after dinner. Every harvest, family relationships were further solidi-fied to last a lifetime.

Drawing from those years of memories, I reconfigure my packing operation. Childhood memories guide the location of a roller or how I'll stack empty boxes for the packers. I rely on family traditions to devise a workable system. I recall Mom's concern for meticulous detail. I place empty boxes precisely within her reach; I prop open the boxes of pads for her daily in-ventory. I realize Dad must be a whole-brain thinker. Before making suggestions, he first scrutinizes my system, the trans-porting of fruit from the fields to shed, the sorting and handling of the delicate produce while packing, and the delivery and shipping of the final product. I won't need my cousins or nieces or nephews. Marcy and the kids might help, but my parents will provide the veteran skills I'll need for my small operation.

The next day my folks come over to review the setup, and we quickly slip into the old roles. Mom takes charge of organizing her packing station, asking, "Where do I toss the culls? How do you want the packing pads stored? What kind of pack are you looking for?"

I slow her down, reminding her I envision a few hundred flats per season, not per day. She ignores me and proceeds to stake out her territory. She is once again matriarch of the pack-ing shed, queen and court simultaneously.

Dad checks my system of picking and hauling in the fruit from the orchard. He has learned to keep his distance from Mom's domain, his turf lying in the fields. He inspects our ladders. I expect him to select his favorite one, but instead he takes four home to tighten the rungs. Like a professional, he readies the team's equipment before the game begins.

Dad and Mom never mention anything about getting paid. They too know the pain of watching good fruits drop to the ground, homeless, with no one wanting them. We work in a partnership, not for the money or even to save these peaches but for family.

I try to rationalize that my folks enjoy finding a new role on this farm, rediscovering their place here, contributing their skills and expertise. Yet it's not quite that simple. I sense an additional significance, something about being a seasoned team that only comes from years and years of working together. We're veterans at being a family.

The shed will include a collection of the new and the old. Instead of a rubber stamp and ink pad, I plan to use a glue gun to attach my own fruit label to the boxes. I design a simple label on my computer and produce copies on a laser printer.

The fruit will still be cleaned first with an old machine from an earlier generation of home packing, a wonderfully efficient and simple device we call a defuzzer. It does just what it says. Through a series of spinning brushes it gently wipes the fuzz off the peach, along with dust and leaves. I have thought about leaving some of the fuzz on as proof that these peaches are organic, fulfilling the image that "natural" means rough. But once defuzzed, the reds and yellows of Sun Crest appear more like a blush, a rouge for these wonderful-tasting peaches, appealing to the eye, attracting those who believe that appearance is part of good taste.

I know of the defuzzer because I recall watching Dad make one. We were a young family then, struggling financially, and

Dad's engineering and design skills were really put to the test, requiring him to copy or invent machines we couldn't afford. The family didn't know if his version worked better or worse than a commercial model, we never got the chance to compare. Instead, his creation became our standard, and as far as we were concerned it was the best. It was "good enough." Our father had built it and that's all that mattered. I grew up working with machines that often had an imprint of family.

But now I cannot locate a commercially manufactured defuzzer. I believe the machine has become obsolete—older, fuzzier varieties of peaches having been replaced by new varieties that do not require as much defuzzing. A shiny and smooth peach has evolved and become the industry standard, and the packing houses have responded with new wash baths instead of defuzzers.

I recall seeing an old defuzzer someplace, perhaps in a neighbor's shed. For days I keep trying to imagine the shed where I had seen it. Finally I ask Dad what happened to our old one, and he says he sold it when he decided to stop home packing.

I know of that decision because I was the cause of it. We stopped packing our own fruit when all the children left the farm. I was the youngest and the last to leave, becoming an idealistic college student at Berkeley who longed for adventure and an escape from the provincial life of rural California. Dad responded to his changing family by sending his peaches to a commercial packing shed.

He sold the defuzzer to a Japanese American farmer in a neighboring community who has since passed away. His widow believes the defuzzer was then resold to another Japanese farmer, although she can't recall exactly who. I begin visiting the Japanese farmers in the area who once packed their own fruit. We talk of the fruit harvests of the past. Some remember the shipping dock in Fresno and watching me grow up through the years. I too remember the scene: Dad talking with his comrades about work and fruit prices while I shared a Pepsi with other farm kids who also tagged along with their fathers and received an end-of-another-workday reward of soda water.

One of these neighbors still farms but no longer packs his fruit. I phone and inquire about his old packing shed. He says he will be happy to show me the operation. As I drive into his yard I spy a shed full of old equipment that looks as if it has not been moved for twenty years. Spiderwebs and layers and layers of dust date the objects. Everything seems to be standing in the exact location as when the family stopped home packing. My suspicions are validated when the old farmer locates hidden electric cords, plugs in the motors, and flicks obscure switches. His smooth gestures suggest that his actions are still routine, habitual behavior from daily chores during summers of harvests. I hear a rumble of chain drives as a giant twelve-foot-diameter packing turntable begins to shake off a layer of caked dust and dirt and a conveyor belt struggles to break loose from hardened rubber drums. The brushes and vacuum motor of a defuzzer churn with new life.

The whine of the machine sounds familiar. I ask where he got the defuzzer or if he made it. He shows me a machine he did make, standing outside, covered with a weathered and torn tarp. Proudly he says, "That is one of the very first models ever made. I invented it. Your dad came over to see this, you know."

He explains that the one currently in his shed was bought from another farmer. Used equipment frequently journeys from family to family, often within a community of relatives or friends. As I examine the machine more closely, the switch looks like the same one I once worked with. Even the waste bag is familiar, a yellowed white rice sack with a faded red rose print and black lettering. One of my jobs was to periodically untie the waste bag and dump it in the fields. This bag is attached to an old rain-gutter drain, just like the one on my folks' house. I am positive this machine is the one Dad made until I recall who built my dad's house. The contractor was a Japanese American who built most of the Japanese American houses in this area; he probably used the same rain gutters on all of them, so this attachment could have come from any home within the community.

I buy the conveyor belts, turntable, rollers, and defuzzer from the neighbor, and he smiles at finally reclaiming his shed. Dad inspects everything as I unload the truck. I pause to study the defuzzer with him, asking if it looks familiar. I anticipate he'll look for a subtle mark, a hidden nail left behind as an artist's signature, a distinct welding bead he alone recognizes as his own.

But Dad can't say for sure and moves on to study the other old equipment. "Thirty years is a long time," he comments. "Besides, it's yours now."

As I position the defuzzer along with the rest of the home packing line, Dad and I tell stories about picking and packing peaches. Marcy, Nikiko, and even little Korio listen and want to help. Niki asks if she has a job, and I picture her as my floor manager in charge of quality control. She'll chastise Baachan for trying to sneak in marginal fruit, reminding us of a new style of management; in Nikiko's language, "The eater is always right." Korio quickly turns his attention to the rollers and plays with the spinning wheels, trying to get them all whirling before the first one stops. I know the game well. Playing on the farm remains equally as important as the work. I will introduce Marcy to another aspect of our family farm and she will see another side of me. The lines between home and work blur as I foresee her becoming my head packer. The presence of my family adds another generation to this farm and creates a new family of memories.

Perhaps salvation for my peaches will become a family affair.

# chapter eight

# wild walks

## *Walking a Field*

I call them farm walks or walking a field, but they're not what most people would imagine. My daily trudges through the farm begin with a specific task such as tramping through a vineyard to fix a broken wire or spot-checking an orchard for worm damage. As I march down a vine row or move from tree to tree I can't help but monitor the life around me: the new leaves, the fruit size and stage of development, the cover-crop growth and the location of weeds, the relationship between ground moisture, weak soils, and stressed plants.

I'll usually carry a shovel and impulsively start cutting sucker growth from vines and tree trunks or begin a never-ending battle against weeds. My walking pace slows and my focus shifts to a micro level. I examine the humus and mulch layers for spiders and study the life on the undersides of leaves. I notice gray ants are everywhere.

As I wonder why the ants scour the trees and vines, my imagination balloons into worry and fear. The ants seem content to wander in the leaf canopies; they run from me and don't bite. I haven't heard of any peach-eating ant species, at least not while the fruit is still attached to the tree and green and growing. I call Pat, my entomologist friend, and he is equally excited but with a scientist's sense of mission. I just want to know what the hell ants are doing in my trees.

Pat believes these ants are preying on worms and other pests. To test his hypothesis, he superglues a worm larva onto a stem. The glue keeps the worm from scurrying away. A gray ant arrives and tries to pull the worm down the tree into the colony. Unable to budge the worm, the ant calls in reinforcements. A company of five ants frantically pull and pull until they rip the larva in two, part of the creature remaining glued to the twig. The rest is carried off for dinner, a truly portable feast.

Pat's story intrigues me. We conclude that the ants are friendly and I should quell my nightmares of killer insect armies ravishing my fields. Now, when I walk, I see the ants as my conservation partners, along with the trees and spiders. I also chuckle, thinking about Pat's creative use of superglue.

### Family Heirs

Not that there aren't horror stories on the farm. They involve nature, though not an ant invasion or a killing frost in spring. Instead, these farm tragedies ensue from a tangle of human nature and inheritance.

I hear of a kind old farmer who leaves his farm to his children, and a Japanese American King Lear drama unfolds. Only one son wants to farm, and he already lives on and works the land while taking care of the folks. But the land is legally in all four of the children's names and the other three want out.

"Sell the farm," they say.

The son who wants to farm cannot afford to buy out the others. The story begins with the end, the inheritance of a farm generating disagreement and division within a family. The land eventually loses its family title.

Tradition from Japan would have given the land to the eldest son, who is obligated to stay and care for his aging parents. For my parents' generation, the Nisei, such traditions were carried out more often than not. Many number-one sons did forsake a career. Some speak with regret about lost dreams of electronics or business and the fact they were never given a choice. They were born expected to stay on the farm.

But for my generation, the Sansei, America's education system has worked all too well. With a promise of mobility and opportunity, most of us left the farm for college and advanced education and now work away from the land. The family farm remained so in name only. At some point, those of us who stayed behind face the issue of land ownership and our futures. Most of the younger farmers delay confrontation with siblings and allow fate to dictate inheritance.

Not I. I ask too many questions. I wonder if I should buy the land from my dad and protect my long-term interests. Should we form a partnership or corporation? How do my brother and sister fit in the picture? Then I hear another King Lear story about a family breaking up over the distribution of a farm estate (I side with the one who stays on the farm and imagine an evil seed growing within the rest of the family). I then devise a plan to lock in a fair market price for the land, with an equitable payment schedule to the family. Dad asks why he can't just give it to me all at one time. I try to explain the tax consequences and bring up the issue of potential inequity for my brother and sister.

He says, "But they're not farming."

In order to buy the farm, I don an estate planner's hat. But I fear the moment I begin thinking of my vines and orchards as commodities with estate tax ramifications. I know that if I put on a businessman's hat, it won't take long to realize that there are a hell of a lot better ways to make money than working with nature to produce a product with fluctuating prices and no job security!

So I farm with my farmer's hat and plan with an estate planner's hat. I work the books with a businessman's hat and occasionally play lawyer with a hat to protect myself from bad people. I have to admit it can be fun wearing hats for careers I'll never have.

When I decided to return to the farm from college, my parents warned me, "You'll be cash poor but land rich."

At the time, I didn't know what they meant. It sounded like a student's life, substituting land for knowledge. Now, a decade later, I've gradually paid off more and more of the farm and have devised a long-term estate plan with my parents. My parents' wills reflect their initial warning about being "land rich." I get the remaining farmland and my sister and brother get the cash.

## Land Claims

Our family didn't own land until after World War II. Few Japanese Americans did. In America it was a bad time to be Japanese. First, the Issei could not buy land (the Alien Land Law of 1913 had singled out all "Orientals" and barred them from owning land). But their children, the Nisei, born in America and thus citizens, could. However, when the Great Depression descended, all families struggled and dreams of land ownership were dashed.

Dad tells the family story: "Just when we were getting back on our feet, all us brothers old enough to work and save a little, the damned war started."

Bad timing and the wrong face. Japanese Americans looked like the enemy who bombed Pearl Harbor. As wartime hysteria grew, we were singled out as a threat to national security. Suddenly Japanese American farmers were perceived as taking over certain agricultural industries. It was imagined that Japanese American fishing communities were potential ports of entry for the enemy. Buddhist churches and Japanese language schools were thought to be strongholds for spies and fifth column activities. Dreams of buying a family farm died.

Over 120,000 Americans of Japanese ancestry, the majority of whom were American citizens by birth, were uprooted and forced to live in isolated camps scattered across the western states in desolate locations. They were imprisoned for four to five years, living behind barbed wire, yet none were ever convicted of sabotage or of aiding the enemy. Many helped in the Allied war effort, bought war bonds, or worked making Allied camouflage, and thousands volunteered to fight the Axis enemy, some of whom formed the 442nd infantry battalion, which became the most highly decorated unit in U.S. military history. My grandparents lost their eldest son, George, in the war. I have a snapshot of his funeral and often stare at the silent and still faces, trying to make sense of the expressions frozen in the snapshot. Baachan lifts a photo of her dead son dressed in his military uniform. Jiichan's hands are loosely holding the tightly folded American flag. The aunts and uncles gather to the side; they look uncomfortable, cramped next to one another, unsure about their hands. Dad remains in the back, his face blurred in

the shadows. While Uncle George fought in Europe and died
for freedom, his family lived behind barbed wire with tens of
thousands of others in the desert of Arizona.

When World War II entered the final days, the military
began closing the relocation camps and issuing tickets to return
home. My grandparents were confused. Three sons were either
dead or still in the military. Another son and a daughter, hungry
to begin their own lives, had left the relocation camps months
earlier when the government opened zones for Japanese American travel. Only my one aunt, a bubbly young teenager, was still
with my grandparents. But Jiichan had grown weak and was an
aging farmworker. The average age of the Issei when they were
evacuated was between fifty and sixty. Baachan remained be-
wildered. She spoke no English. The family was broke. Now
the government demanded they again relocate by "going
home."

My grandparents were one of the last families to leave camp.
They had no farm, they had no home. Given little choice, they
asked for a ticket back to Selma, California, their last address.
Others more fortunate, especially those with property, had already returned to their homes but often discovered vandalism
and possessions missing. Some found their farmhouses had
mysteriously burned in their absence.

One Nisei woman tells of a missing tea set. Her mother was
outspoken for an Issei and insisted on inquiring about the lost
set, dragging the Nisei daughter along to act as translator. Their
Caucasian neighbor shook her head and had no idea concerning
the disappearance. Instead she invited the two in for refresh-
ments. When they had tea, the Japanese American mother and
daughter discovered their missing property.

"Did your mother say anything?" I ask.

"No," says the Nisei daughter, "I couldn't believe it, either.
During the whole visit, Mom just sat there, tight-lipped, and occasionally sipped some of her tea."

A few lucky Japanese American farmers had good neighbors, good people who managed farms for their interned friends. There's little documentation of their acts; usually it was an agreement sealed with a handshake between neighbors. These farmers were called "Jap lovers."

A good neighbor named Kamm Oliver explains. "We didn't have a lease or anything written. I just sent the Hiyamas a check at the end of the year. There was some back talk for a while . . . but what the heck, it was the decent thing to do. I was raised to treat others as I'd like to be treated . . . our families were good friends. Yeah, I tried to farm their place just like it was mine."

A family friend wrote to Jiichan and Baachan before they returned to Selma and said they could stay at their empty grocery store for a few months until the store could be reopened. So the family returned, veterans from a different war, and faced a new battle in the fields of California.

I imagine that returning was like emigrating once again, arriving in a land as a foreigner with nothing. However, it was a lifetime later, and among their possessions was a life history of shattered dreams.

Dad became head of the household, laboring in the fields and leasing some land. Then, tired of working for someone else, he risked all his savings and purchased a farm.

Baachan objected. "We can't afford a farm. Can't take the gamble. Can't take risk in America."

But Dad figured, What the hell, what have I got to lose? If we don't make it, we're just back where we started.

As I DREAM and plan to make the farm my own, I have inherited this family history as my legacy, part of the baggage that comes with my land. After hearing these stories, I can't help but be aware of them each year and each season. They have become part of the farm landscape.

*Wild Walks*

With harvest a few weeks away, my farm walks acquire a wild
pace. Changes unfold daily: the peaches swell, fresh green
shoots continually reach for sunlight, the weeds race to flower.
If I stop to check a tree or a branch, throngs of insects and spiders greet me. I make up names for them: "the little jumpy spider with an attitude problem," "the hard-shelled black beetle
from a Nintendo game," "the flying critters that move so fast it's
hard to even tag them with a nickname."

Even the dirt seems to change daily. Moisture in the soil is
quickly sucked out by the tree roots and by our 100-degree summer days and 70-degree nights. The air becomes parched and so
dry that on many mornings dew does not visit. I try to monitor
the soil dehydration by shades of color, from the lush dark
chocolate brown of mud to the leathery tan of drying topsoil
and the bleached silt that cracks in our native desert heat.

But my eyes deceive me, for I need to know what's going on
below the surface, where the roots lie. I consider buying an expensive tensiometer, a shiny metal stake I can jam into the earth
that reads moisture levels. Then a neighbor tells me how much
soils differ from one end of the farm to the other. Even around
a tree, the earth varies and distorts moisture readings, com-
pounded by human error when someone digs a few inches
deeper or shallower with each sample.

As an experiment, I poke a skinny metal pipe next to one tree
and hit a root about eighteen inches down. In another spot my
probe doesn't penetrate beyond two feet and gets stuck, and I
have to use a shovel to dig it out. My soil must be extremely
compacted but the tree doesn't seem to mind, it stands flush
with growth and bears a heavy crop. So I resort to using the old
farmer method of moisture testing. I dig and grab a handful of

dirt and squeeze it. If the earth sticks together without crum-
bling there's probably enough dampness without stressing the
tree or vine. If it doesn't hold together, I might start to think
about watering soon.

An uneasiness accompanies my preharvest walks. Thoughts
of the potential price of peaches start to disturb my vision of natural farming. The two coalesce as uneasy bedfellows, a blend of
bottom-line thinking driven by economics jumbled with believing in one's work as something beyond monetary value. I can
rationalize lousy prices as part of a yeoman's lifestyle, but I also
know good prices make work a whole lot more fun. The roller-
coaster ride toward harvest begins.

My imagination runs rampant with fears: a just-before-
harvest freak storm or an attack of a killer monster worm. I succumb to a type of humility, a fragile balance between the
controlled and uncontrolled. I conclude, "We farmers do not
rule over our lands."

Farmers fool themselves when they talk about taking land
from the wild. Some believe they can outwit nature and grow a
lush vineyard in poor soils and on land where vines don't belong. But I sense that farming is only a temporary claim on a
piece of earth, not a right; farmers borrow the land from nature
to squeeze out a living.

With each generation we may be losing that sense of "claiming the land." Armed with our machinery and with youthful
confidence, we've never felt nature beat us. In the end, though,
nature has a way of keeping us in our place by a thunderstorm
on our table grapes, a heat wave that burns the peaches, or
showers that fall on unprotected grapes trying to dry into
raisins. We are humbled.

WHEN MY WALKS take me to Dad's "hill," I am reminded of
our family's claim to that ten acres of land and how nature almost broke a farmer's will. The hill was a rise on the landscape, a

mound of dirt with a hidden layer of hardpan a few feet beneath it. The original vines on this patch of land were weak, their frail root systems stunted by the hardpan and poor drainage. The land could not support life, so large areas were not planted and stood barren. But it was the hill and the hardpan that made this farm affordable and attractive to a young man with little cash and a hunger to work the land.

Hardpan is missing from the rock charts of a regular geology lesson. It is a compacted layer of clay and minerals, impervious to roots, more stone than anything else. Farmers swear hardpan was created to break their backs and protect the hills of the San Joaquin Valley from vineyards and orchards, nature's revenge against man's tillage. In the Northeast, farmers made their fences out of fieldstones. In Del Rey they used hardpan.

Dad's hill was a solid hardpan layer with a thin but rich skin of topsoil. In order to farm this land, tons and tons of rocks had to be hauled away and disposed of. The hill had to be leveled, making a flat plateau for irrigating crops. Dad first called in a pair of giant Caterpillar tractors, which rumbled across his land. They ripped out the meager vines that had been trying for decades to gain a foothold in the rock. The weak plants resembled coastal Monterey pines clinging to a sea cliff embankment. The vineyard looked aesthetically powerful, the vines tenaciously defying nature and surviving the challenge, but they produced few if any grapes.

The thundering machines tossed the vines aside and attacked the hardpan. It was man versus rock, and the rocks grudgingly gave up ground. The hill was partially leveled, flattened, and ripped, but it teemed with huge blocks of hardpan, like a pot of chili teeming with beans, more beans than beef, more hardpan than soil.

So Dad spent his fall, winter, spring, and summer clearing his field, lifting the chunks of rock one by one, lugging them away, and tossing them onto his old flatbed truck, day after day, truckload after truckload. Some of the hardpan was stubborn, huge plates of rock, thousands of pounds lodged beneath other chunks. His main weapons were a strong back, a fierce hunger to farm that hill, and dynamite.

Mom wasn't fond of the dynamite. With each explosion she shook from the blasting noise and fear for her husband's safety. The dynamite blew apart the plates, making a sea of smaller pieces that could be lifted and dragged to the truck. Day after day, truckload after truckload.

Dad lost a year of planting, refusing to plant vines in the rocky soil of that field. Once all the surface rocks were cleared he called back the Caterpillars and ripped the earth again. A huge shank sliced the ground, tearing at hidden layers of hardpan, breaking the rock's domain. His formerly clean field disappeared. New chunks of hardpan surfaced and blanketed the land, popping up in the earth as if they floated on water in the wake of the Caterpillars. The mission began again, lugging and tossing. But this time he used less dynamite and the rocks were smaller, averaging only a few pounds each. Dad went through fewer pairs of gloves this second round, too, and a sense of progress was felt.

Now a healthy, strong vineyard stands on the hill. The vines are vigorous, the roots penetrating and secure. Occasionally, while Dad disks or cultivates, a chunk of hardpan surfaces. He stops the tractor and carries the rock to the end of the row, where a small collection stands.

"They seem to keep growing," he explains. "But so do the vines. So do the vines."

I'll consider myself a better farmer when I have a clearer sense of history about a place, when I understand the knowledge of a farm's hills and the sweat and blood left behind. Until then I'm just managing a piece of dirt and probably still foolishly believing I rule the earth.

M Y  F A R M  W A L K S slow as I sense the surrounding life: the lush green canopy of peaches and the scent of ripening fruit and the soft matting of lavish cover crop underfoot. My farm's cornucopia is overflowing with insect and spider families that seem ubiquitous. The farm seems out of control, and suddenly I'm amazed I can even harvest a crop. To be truthful, I know very little about how a peach actually grows. I do a few things out in the fields and *voilà!* a peach. Nature must be on my side, I'm lucky to get a crop in year after year.

I get superstitious in late summer. With harvest so close I try not to do things out of the ordinary. I talk out loud a lot, as if I'm bargaining with nature. I'll ask the weather to cooperate, the worms to hold off a few weeks, the trees to pump up the fruit a little bigger this year, the vines to avoid water stress until after harvest. I feel grateful.

Most people think farmers give thanks after harvest, like the Pilgrims. I believe right before harvest, when the farm is the most vulnerable and exposed, we become the most grateful. I'm humbled to realize in a few hours or days an entire crop can be lost. My gratitude becomes an act of submission as well as a type of freedom. I'm guided by an absolute faith in nature during the final hours preceding harvest. Instead of problems to solve, I can work only in awe of the natural mystery of farming.

## Baachan Walks

She may appear at any time and place, most often late in the day, during an evening walk by myself or with my family. My senses play tricks with my imagination. A tree casts an odd shadow, and out of the corner of my eye I think I see someone. Or the grape leaves rustle and I believe I hear the sound of footsteps. I imagine someone escorting me, and for a second I envision Baachan walking the farm.

I remember Baachan. As if walking against the wind, she would slouch forward and plod along the earthen trail. Baachan often sang to herself, more of a chant than a song, childlike in its melody.

*"Pen, pen, pen . . . po, po, po, . . . pen, pen, po, po."*

Her frail eighty-year-old legs would shuffle through the soft dirt, creating puffs of dust that marked her trail. She'd clasp her hands behind her, shoulders round, and droop toward the earth, her tiny frame silhouetted against a brilliant orange setting sun.

I can picture her trudging through the fields she worked but never owned. Yet I believe that despite a life of poverty and the crushing upheaval of the World War II relocation, in her old age she found peace during those farm walks, covering familiar territory and finding a place where she belonged.

*chapter nine*

# harvests

## Finding a Home

In the early morning sunrise, I stand out on the porch. Despite the heat of summer, a chill greets me as the sun peeks over the Sierras, but the coolness quickly retreats with the heat of the first rays. I can hear a neighbor's tractor and his workers beginning their day. I'm excited and relieved that harvest will soon begin. Is this what it's like to start labor and birth? Impatient to end the nine-month ordeal, yet anxious about beginning a new life as a parent, knowing nothing may ever be the same?

With the aroma of ripening fruit at harvest, my senses detect a subtle fragrance lingering in the air, much like the delicate perfume of a passing woman, tantalizing the imagination long after she has departed.

A week earlier the fragrance caught my attention. I stopped to examine peaches from the outside trees, which ripen before the rest of the field because of their extra helping of unfiltered sunlight. I squeeze one with an amber hue. It has a slight give, telling me it is almost ready and that the majority of the field will soon follow. Unable to resist the scent, I pick and bite a crunchy peach. Immediately the taste jumps out and dances on my tongue. This is why I work to save this peach: Sun Crests have flavor!

As the day unfolds, temperatures rocket into the 90s, then even higher. Plants wilt as the thermometer pushes near 100. Heat rises off the earth's surface in visible ripples. Radio talk shows advertise contests, listeners guessing which day we will break 100. I do my best to remain cool, knowing dozens of 100-degree days will arrive and scorch the valley. But peaches love the dry heat. They gulp water, double in size, and break color with tinges of red showing like a blush. Harvest is near.

When I walk through my fields of Sun Crest, adrenaline starts to flow. Harvesttime approaches with excitement and the spirit of a chase. I have succeeded in finding a new way to grow these peaches; now my quest remains—to find a home for them.

I devise two strategies. First I will personally choose the best fruit and ship it to specialty markets, where buyers are willing to pay for the quality. The second strategy rests with a new baby food company I hear about from some farmer friends. This company's buyer claims to want my peaches. I begin both with a farmer's skepticism.

Peaches are picked in "rounds," beginning at the top of the tree, where the fruit ripens first. Pickers work their way down a tree with each round. Three to four times we will enter a field, glean the best, and leave the rest to mature and grow. It may take up to two weeks to complete the harvest. The first round produces some of the best fruit, though it's expensive for a large crew to harvest them. Most of a laborer's time is spent moving from branch to branch and tree to tree, searching for the ripe fruit. Yet these first gems will work well for a small-scale premium fruit round. I make plans to renew the family packing operation.

Dad and I wake early and start the harvest. We pick the first buckets slowly, not used to being so selective. We have different picking styles. Color is not necessarily the best indicator for maturity, even though most people judge produce solely with their eyes. Dad uses a combination of color and feel he can't exactly describe to me. I use a gentle squeeze method: if the fruit gives a little, then it's ripe. It reminds me of working with clay and ceramics, where you develop a tactile sense as you pull the clay into a cylinder and push it out into a shape, a vessel. I explain my method to Dad and he listens patiently as he picks, continuing with the style he's developed from years of work in the fields. I notice he has almost twice as many buckets picked as I do. His method takes into account the cost-of-time factor, something the clay artist in me didn't consider.

By midmorning I spy Mom walking over to the shed. She slips into her old role of head packer. I bring peaches to the shed and she proceeds to separate them by size and pack them into boxes. I have to slow her down and explain that I'm trying to market these fruits for very particular buyers.

"Only the very, very best," I caution. "The slightest defect is a cull. Remember, people are willing to pay good money for these jewels."

She nods, but I know she'll try to cheat. Old habits are hard to break.

I understand her thinking. Often the slightly misshapen or unevenly colored peaches are still wonderful. When we packed our own fruit years ago, our goal was to produce a good quality box, but no better than we had to because buyers were not going to reward us for anything extra special. Consumers seem to shop with an attitude of spending as little as possible on food. "Good enough" is the rule. But this specialty market is for a new kind of consumer, exclusive buyers willing to spend money for the best.

Later Marcy and the kids come out to join us. For a moment we step back in time and become that farm family I remember. The grown-ups chat as we work and the kids play in the dirt. The dog, Jake, lies at my feet while I sort the peaches. Mom sighs at seeing the wonderful fruits being culled and decides to set them aside for neighbors. In the afternoon she'll make her rounds, giving away delicious peaches and visiting friends she hasn't seen in months. Marcy will spend the rest of the day canning and making jam with these fruits, trying to capture the flavor and preserve the taste for cold winter mornings. The scene might be from a Norman Rockwell painting, except with a Japanese American farming family.

I call my specialty fruits "dessert peaches." Some will be used by chefs featuring seasonal and regional cuisines for their summer desserts. Others are to go to a southern California hotel that plans to leave peaches instead of chocolates for their patrons when the beds are turned down in the evenings. I joke to Marcy that these peaches are bound for no one we know. She quips that our goal may be to grow peaches none of our friends can afford.

We ship a couple of hundred boxes. I locate another buyer, a high-quality produce store in Berkeley. The problem with these specialty markets is that none of them can handle large quantities, and there's no one to take the rest of my Sun Crests. Exclusive shoppers may love the fruit, and my family certainly enjoys these few days of nostalgic home packing, but eighty tons of Sun Crest continue to ripen.

## Peach Harvest

On the evening before we start the harvest, the orchard bouquet is thick and ubiquitous. We've begun a family ritual, Marcy and I each drive a tractor and bin trailer out to the fields, preparing for the next day's harvest. We each have a child in our lap, and fifty feet from the orchard they too can recognize the scent. It excites all of us, and we salivate in anticipation of plucking juicy treasures from the trees.

We park the trailers in the rows and climb off for our treat. A cloud of peach perfume envelops us as we each silently devour a peach. For our second helping we're more patient and selective. I'll search out some of the overripe ones I've been eyeing each time I've passed the field. These peaches sit fully exposed to the sun or on a lone corner tree that has always ripened first. The ground is a little different under that tree, a bit more sandy, and three sides are exposed to the summer heat. The family gathers as I reach up and pick a gushy entree for each of us.

The juice dribbles off our chins, we suck out the meat and smile with a primeval grin. I revert to childish behavior and allow the flesh to dangle from my teeth.

Niki screams "Gross!" and then sinks her teeth into a peach, trying to imitate her father.

Korio can't understand our words but continues to stuff himself. More meat leaks onto his shirt than down his throat. He pauses as we all stare at him, then continues with a grin half hidden by the candylike pulp. We feast and celebrate the beginning of harvest.

THIS SUMMER I find new hope in a company that buys organic fruit in large quantities. My peaches will become organic baby food.

A farmer friend told me about them. He has been supplying them for years, putting up with their late payments. The baby food company has grown quickly, become better established, and is looking for new growers.

Being a father, I understand parental concern for the diet of infants. My organic certification ensures against harmful chemicals or residues. I can also imagine infants championing the cause of those farmers who work with, not against, nature. I grin at the idea of a nation of babies underwriting a new farming alternative.

I believe in the value of organic baby food. Witnessing the birth of my children, holding their tiny, squirming bodies, was a real turning point in my life. My children provide me with perspective. I do not farm solely to make money but rather with the hope of contributing something to them and to the world. The thought of my peaches feeding infants and toddlers adds to my satisfaction. This summer will be a special harvest.

Babies and meals, a time we care about our foods, foods as a part of life. This is how the harvest begins, my fields suddenly connected to kitchens and family dinner tables. I can envision my peaches as part of these scenes, part of these homes. The palates of babies could save my Sun Crests.

IN YEARS PAST, I've been punished for picking ripe fruit for the fresh market. My Sun Crests, of course, don't keep well beyond a week and can't compete with other, newer varieties bred for their color and long shelf life. Marketing and distribution systems just aren't set up for extremely ripe peaches.

Some recently released varieties must be the salesman's ulti-mate dream. They're so red and dark they look ripe all the time, even while green on the tree and immature inside. But I fear the fresh fruit industry is shooting itself in the foot, with farmers planting varieties so red we can't tell if they're ripe until a con-sumer bites into one to find a terrible-tasting fruit. Even pickers often can't distinguish between ones ready for harvest and those that are bitter and need another week on the tree. Instead of a dream fruit, we may be creating a monster.

When the workers arrive that first harvest morning, I tell them to harvest only the ripe fruits that have a red-yellow color. I wish I could speak better Spanish. I want to tell them, Pick the fruit with the rich amber glow of harvesttime.

The workers are not used to working with such mature fruit. Normal harvests are carried out before the fruit softens. They start to discard all the soft ones, dropping them on the ground. I plead with them to save those peaches. This year's harvest can be riper, I explain, nearly overripe and bursting with natural flavor. They look at me oddly as I explain that the gushy ones are the best. I offer them bites of a ripe peach, and they have to lean over before the juice oozes down their faces. They grin, and I sense we now understand each other.

Ordinarily when I pick for the fresh peach market, I haul the fruit to a local packing shed. But this year's Sun Crests need to be transported to a processing plant, where they will be pureed. Large transport trucks will pick them up and haul them away. Every driver gets lost trying to find my farm.

"Why don't you have your name and address on the road-side? You need a big sign," one protests. I look at the map I sent him, lying on the truck seat, crumpled and torn. Somehow I doubt he'd understand that the last thing I want is to put a big sign out on the road.

The driver cusses and swears he'll never come out to my

place again. I quickly step away from his rig. I imagine being chased by a wild truck driver carrying out his ultimate revenge on farmers with no roadside address numbers. The trucker's face is beet red from the 100-degree heat, and I suggest some cool water would be refreshing. As he dips his entire head under the garden hose and the blood drains from his complexion, I remember why we have no sign on the roadside. I enjoy the seclusion. I can hide on my farm.

THIS SEASON, BECAUSE my peaches are destined for infants, I acquire a different type of pride in my work because it's done "for the babies." Every day during our harvest, my own two-year-old taste-tests the peaches. I know they've passed his inspection when the front of his shirt is stained pink. I take off his shirt, and Jake licks the juice off my son's face and chest. When Korio giggles and Jake wags his tail, I know these peaches are ripe and ready.

I feel a wonderful sense of fulfillment. But I have only a single-year contract with the baby food company, and I remind myself that next year will probably be very different. I am excited about collaborating with them and write to the company about my hope for a long-term contract or a profit-sharing plan. My letter is referred to another department in another state, and later it's returned with a handwritten *no* jotted next to each of my ideas.

But I still enjoy the moment. My homeless peaches have found shelter for this season.

## Harvest Lessons

Every summer, harvests of the past rush through my thoughts. I begin to sound old, recalling my childhood summers and workdays that become hotter and harder every time I retell the stories to my children. I recall the summer of '72, my last farm harvest before college, and my burning desire to escape the farm. I remember the summers spent hauling fruit in from the fields with my brother. We'd drive a tractor and stop where the pickers had stacked wooden boxes full of peaches. We'd each take a side and hoist the crates onto a wagon, hundreds of boxes a day. I don't know why we called this work "swamping"—maybe because the heat and grasses and damp earth all combined to feel like a swamp. The work battered our young bodies. We'd take turns putting our heads under the water faucet at home, trying to cool off and wash away the exhaustion of the summer.

I clearly remember the first time I drove the big truck to haul bins full of fruit to a packing shed miles away. Dad sat next to me, teaching a nervous son how to shift the gears of the Chevy flatbed, sharing his techniques and tricks about how to handle a ten-ton load sitting less than three feet behind you. Later I'd laugh about how anxious I was and how perspiration dotted my forehead and my palms made the steering wheel grimy.

My heart raced, the adrenaline tingled my nerves, my eyes couldn't stay focused on the road and, instead, darted in every direction. There seemed to be so many details to monitor: shifting through eight gear changes; reclutching and adjusting to a hi-low dual rear axle; listening and trying to remember Dad's few words of advice, like "Never hit the brakes." As we neared the first stop sign I understood Dad's warning about braking. The weight of the load makes the truck into a giant rolling snowball. Once we built up speed (grinding through eight gears), man and machine catapulted down the road. I had to ease into the brakes, slowing into a gentle roll. I had to learn a new way to stop.

I cannot recall the precise year—it was sometime after college—when I first hinted to Dad that I might want to farm. I had asked him how I could help with the harvest, so he approached me about handling the workers. It didn't sound complicated. I'd call in the crew to pick the fruit, monitor their work, and then make sure they were paid. But it was my first experience with supervising people, and I found myself unprepared to be promoted to the ranks of management. Dad gave his just-out-of-college liberal son his ultimate lesson: a welcome-to-the-real-world out in the fields, with plenty of opportunities to fail.

I can't recall another summer filled with as much anger and frustration. I became responsible for selecting the day to start picking, determining when the fruit was ripe, and calling in a twenty-man crew. Equipment had to be prepared, bin trailers and tractors readied. After one morning with workers being paid to just stand around as I pleaded with a tractor to start, I learned a new lesson in business management. Half the work is setting up. Once you call in a crew, their hundred-dollars-an-hour meter starts running. Every minute they're in your field costs you. Mistakes become expensive.

I also had to communicate how I wanted the workers to pick. A price was attached to every instruction. If they had to search for just the ripest peaches, costs rose dramatically. Some workers understood my instructions only after I showed them what I wanted. Even then, each worker maintained his individuality and picked in his own style. I learned the lesson of splitting the difference and meeting them halfway. Perfection in farming is unrealistic, be it in nature or human nature.

That summer I learned to live with my mistakes and, perhaps just as important, to feel good about the accomplishments. As the weeks passed I grew more proficient, and Dad monitored my work less and less, his quiet way of giving praise. Then he began asking me what work *I'd* like done. A rite of passage had occurred. I was a real farmer.

I am amazed we make it to harvest. When I think of the many things that can go wrong, I'm grateful for *any* edible fruit. Even with the first picking round under way, I fear that unseen worms are munching my peaches or fungi and bacteria are attacking them like alien invaders. I check the first bins warily, searching for defects. A farmer's pessimism surfaces at harvest, as eyes drift toward the blemishes.

A type of humility marks a real farmer. Those of us who battle nature all year must ultimately accept the hand we're dealt. We're cautious even at harvest, privately smiling when we discover that the cards we hold may be OK, inwardly grateful that there hasn't been a disaster. We hear of someone else with bad luck: a farm caught under a hailstorm, a plum orchard that bore no crop, a vineyard with a mildew outbreak. Success is relative. We pick our fruit and whisper to ourselves, "It could have been worse."

Bitter harvests of the past do not easily fade from memory. Too often I have left fruit on the trees when the market price did not cover the expense of picking. Other years, I harvested solely to reduce losses, trying to recoup expenses already invested in the ripe, juicy peaches. I have also harvested knowing I will lose money.

A city cousin asks, "If the margins are so close, why even pick at all?" He uses a cliché: "Cut your losses."

My cousin cannot comprehend the emotions that ripen with my fruit. At harvesttime I go public. My ego is peddled with my peaches. I risk rejection and am unwilling to admit that no one wants my fruits. Also, because my work is where I live, I pass an unpicked orchard daily. The drive is painful. I sense more than failure, I question my own worth. So sometimes I'll harvest anyway, ignoring the cost and refusing to believe that my work is without value. I'll pick just to clean up an orchard, to get the crop out of sight. With each bad harvest the farmer dies a little.

## Where Good Peaches Come From

Where do all these peaches come from? Surely the truckloads of compost I applied last year do not add up to eighty tons of peaches this year. I begin to total all the ingredients in a juicy peach—water, some pest treatments, the labor of a dozen workers, my own time and management skills—and I still can't equate them with a luscious harvest. Simple linear formulas do not apply in farming. I stumble when I try to analyze the equation for a successful crop, reducing needs into inputs like nitrogen, moisture, and a few sprays. I discover that the process is much more complex. A farmer friend agrees: "Good peaches are more than just dirt, manure, and ditch water."

Reaping a good harvest depends on a marriage of farmer and farm, but the output of a healthy farm extends beyond the individual. I recall many conversations with neighbors as we experiment and try new methods. At times we swap stories and the results of our trials, at others we simply offer encouragement.

I alone cannot claim credit for my peaches. I think of my dad, for he planted this orchard. Peering into the past I also see my grandparents, who journeyed to America, and the generations of farmers in Japan that compose the Masumoto family.

But if I let my imagination run too wild, this familial debt of gratitude can quickly bankrupt me. A good harvest needs to be a time for celebration, not guilt. I remember an old farmer telling me to enjoy the harvest and explaining, "Some farmers simply have more luck than others," then winking at my perplexed expression.

And I underestimate the genius of nature. For months I live and work in the midst of magic, such as the simple power of sunlight and the transformation it causes in plants. Science may call it photosynthesis, transforming light into energy. I call it a gift from nature. My best term to describe this magic is *synergism,* the combining of individual parts to create something greater than the whole. The concept seems baffling. I've been conditioned not to expect something for nothing; everything supposedly has a price. Nature shortchanges herself of recognition by providing us with more than we put in.

My definition of synergism also includes the battles against weeds and pests, for they too integrate into the magic of a good harvest. Are Bermuda grass and peach twig borers part of a juicy peach? The thought challenges my reasoning. It's easier to think in terms of competition or compromise, not a collaborative effort of seemingly chaotic forces.

I ask a scientist, "What makes a good peach?"

He responds with a discussion that focuses on inputs and farming practices, as if a bountiful harvest can be accomplished by technology alone.

He stops talking when I suggest, "I would like to think the farmer also has something to do with it."

## Obon

My Sun Crest harvest corresponds with the season for Obon. Obon is an annual Japanese festival with folk dancing in the streets, a ritual to honor family. Through lively and colorful dance, we perpetuate our ancestors in memory and display gratitude to them. Originating from a blend of folk culture and Buddhist beliefs, Obon celebrates the idea that ancestors return briefly to visit the living, even if only in memory and symbols.

Colorful lanterns light the way for spirits to return home, and the dance symbolizes the joy of this spiritual reunion.

At an Obon, colorful kimonos or *yukata* flash as dancers spin, turn, and dip, their movements free and relaxed. *Kachi-kachi* crack together like castanets and the *taiko* drums beat a rhythm of folk songs. Participants dance in a huge circle. Spectators are encouraged to join, their sometimes rough gestures adding a festive element. Music echoes over the Buddhist church grounds, a magical blend of Japanese song and dance against the backdrop of a summer evening.

It's a fusion of motion and spirit. An illusion is created—the entire community dances, including the blurred image of a great-grandfather or -grandmother dancing as he or she once may have done. Obon is a time of celebration and rejoicing.

The Issei brought Obon with them to America. For these struggling pioneers, toiling for long hours and low pay in the vineyards and orchards of California, Obon broke the monotony, re-creating a slice of homeland in the San Joaquin Valley. For the Nisei it provided a grand opportunity to meet other Japanese farm kids, or, as a Nisei woman explained, "one of the few times for the boys to visit with the girls." Once, dozens of Japanese American communities in small towns throughout the valley held their own Obon. Now the number is reduced, but the celebration of history is still renewed annually with a new generation of dancers.

I'm transported back into this history during the Obon. I can recall wandering amid the dancers as an infant, anticipating my summer treat of a shaved-ice *azuki*—sweetened Japanese red beans in syrup over ice chips. As a teenager I would visit with other farm kids, finding mutual comfort as we compared notes of long workdays on our farms and then enjoyed a summer evening of street dancing. On the day of the Obon, our family used to quit picking fruit early. We'd escape briefly from work to celebrate the harvest, Sun Crest and Obon joined together in mutual celebration.

Even now, between the lively music and the spinning and whirling dancers, I sometimes imagine I can see the ghosts of my grandmother and grandfather. They come to dance with me and my children.

# chapter ten

# september is not
# to be trusted

## Dance with Nature

"Diversify" remains the golden rule for small farms. We assume a defensive posture and protect ourselves against marginal years by raising more than one crop. For my father, this meant growing both peaches and grapes. In his later years, he took it a step further. The majority of our grapes would still be dried into raisins, but he also signed a contract for some to be crushed for juice and wine. He grew weary of battling weather hostile to raisin drying. At least grapes for juice don't mind an occasional September rain.

I inherit his cautious attitude and doom myself to a life of cutting losses instead of maximizing profits. But I can see why the golden rule survives. Nature weeds out speculators who expect quick profits from farming. Some years my peaches support the grapes and in other years the opposite. The few times both have sold well call for celebration; the times both sour make me happy I can start each year anew.

I dance with nature and we seem to constantly be switching leads. Huge rewards may not await me, but perhaps it's the music and motion that's important. I've survived at farming for a decade and now know diversity results in this: at the end of each song, I still have hope.

## Raisins, a Family Affair

At the end of every summer, when it's time to harvest the raisins, I step back in time. Making raisins follows old rituals begun at the turn of the century. The industrial revolution and the miracles of technology have bypassed raisin vineyards. Green grapes are still picked in early September and spread out on trays that lie directly on the earth, exposed to the elements. A waiting game commences, and, as they have for generations, farmers pray for pale blue skies and hot days. Eyes turn to the west, scanning the horizon for approaching storms. Within twenty days the sun dries the grapes into dark, sweet raisins, a simple and natural process done entirely without equipment, machinery, or technology. I still make raisins in essentially the same way that my dad and his dad did.

Since the first raisin crop in the late 1800s, the harvest has undergone only one major change. The two-by-three-foot trays used to be made of wood; today most everyone uses trays of paper. Wooden trays worked well for decades, their flat wide panels strong and reusable, and the grapes dried quickly and cleanly. But the bulky wooden trays required tremendous amounts of hand labor, as they were passed out into the fields, collected at the end of the drying season, and stored for next year. Because an average acre produces between a ton and two tons of raisins and uses from five hundred to a thousand trays for each acre, even a small farm requires tens of thousands of trays. The introduction of paper trays was driven by convenience and led to huge stacks of abandoned wooden ones.

Family has always played a role in making raisins. Local rural districts used to delay the start of the school year to allow families to pick grapes. Children understood that a good harvest meant new school clothes. Like a pilgrimage, aunts, uncles, and cousins returned to the old home place to help with the harvest. Farmers enjoyed the advantages of their large extended families.

Our family used to work together as a team. Armed with their knives, Dad and Mom slashed away at the hanging bunches, dropping them into a large grape pan shaped like a deep pie dish. We kids crawled on our knees on smooth packed earth already warming in the hot summer sun. Our job was to lay out trays between the rows. Then, after my folks would dump their pans of grapes, we'd spread them into an even layer on each tray.

Now mostly men harvest the raisins. Occasionally, though, the tradition of families and raisin picking continues (despite labor laws prohibiting children from working). Families hungry for work will sneak their children into the fields, with parents picking and children spreading the grapes. Later the younger children will spend the afternoon napping under a vine.

After grapes are picked and spread, a marathon wait begins that tests my patience. Slowly the green grapes wither, and a light purple hue is reflected from the dehydrating berries. I grow anxious. Eventually the top side of the bunch dries.

Now each trayful is turned or flipped over. Two workers, one at each end of a tray, bend over, place an empty tray on top of the partially dried grapes, and, with good timing and a quick flip, turn the entire tray. Good turning teams work quickly and smoothly, their teamwork marked by a steady, unbroken rhythm. Bad teams are sloppy: the raisins fly and trays are crumpled and twisted, with grapes resting in piles instead of making even layers. Some people can work alone, using fast hands, good timing, and a steady cadence.

Finally the grapes become raisins, dark and meaty, the sun a wonderfully inexpensive dehydrator. Trays are then rolled like a cigarette, or with a few folds, a biscuit roll is created, the raisins wrapped safely inside. Teams then begin boxing by dumping the raisins out of the rolls into boxes or bins.

When I was a child, my family worked as a team to box the raisins. I drove the tractor, pulling a wagon between the vine rows. My parents picked up the raisin rolls and dumped them into wooden boxes destined for processing plants like Sun Maid or Del Monte. Trailing the wagon, my brother and sister collected the used paper trays and burned them in small piles.

Sun-drying raisins is one of the few practices no one has found a way to do better, and I hope, for the sake of the family raisin farmer, that they never do.

Raisins and family. The relationship is tested when an advancing rainstorm threatens to rot a drying raisin crop or a scorching summer heat of 105 degrees bakes grapes into "beans." In a few crucial hours, a family must race to roll up trays before the crop gets wet or too dry, trying to protect the year's investment of labor. We work side by side and familial bonds are forged, everyone sensing the panic. We know that with each minute another few trays can be salvaged.

Even in those families where the children have left the farm, a few will still come home at harvesttime to help their parents.

Others pay extra attention to the weather in September, noticing when a southern storm tracks northward from Baja California or a cold front drops from Alaska into the Central Valley. A rained-out backyard barbecue or tee-off time means more than just a ruined afternoon for adult children of raisin farmers. Calling from distant homes, they act like outposts, warning of approaching fronts in San Diego, Los Angeles, or San Francisco.

An older generation of retired raisin farmers also still retains a keen interest in the annual harvest. I knew of an old Japanese man who, his wife dead, refused to live with his children, not wanting to burden anyone, and stayed on in the family home. But every night during the raisin harvest he'd phone each of his four sons to ask, "How are the raisins?" He still wanted to be involved, to lend moral support. He'd end his conversations with, "Don't work too hard."

One of the sons explained. "I don't mind the calls. It's important when you're old to keep your mind active. It's OK for Dad to worry about the raisins a little."

## September Is Not to Be Trusted

An old-timer says, "September is not to be trusted." He makes raisins and has seen the weather in September take away his year of labor in a single storm. He has fruit trees too and understands how one crop can save another. I had witnessed several disastrous rains while growing up, but only late in my last year of college, when I returned to help my dad on the farm, did I understand what the neighbor meant.

Early one morning I first heard the soft rhythm of morning rain and jumped out of bed to the window. "Damn." Dad's entire crop of grapes lay unprotected on the ground. They needed another week of sun to dry. I turned, hesitated, and said, "Dad, you know it's—"

"I know," he said.

Puddles began to appear in the rows. Fed by clouds, they slowly advanced toward the grape trays. Raisins can tolerate a light rain, but this time, with constant long showers, a year's work began to rot. The stench would soon fill the countryside.

"How bad do you think they are?" I asked.

"We'll see when it stops," Dad answered.

It rained more than an inch. The paper trays seemed to melt, saturated with water. The lower third of each tray became submerged with loose grapes floating in the pools that had formed. I grew restless, hating the sound of the rain.

Dad occasionally glanced out the window, pretending to look for the newspaper or the mail. He spoke little, saying nothing about the harvest lying outside. He spent the day reading old issues of *Popular Mechanics* and some farm magazines. The newspaper had been accidentally thrown into a puddle. "Son of a bitch," he said, returning with the drenched sheets. "At least I want my paper dry."

The rains continued. Dad wrestled with the soaked newspaper, peeling the pages apart and spreading them over chairs to dry. A few years before it had rained like this, over two inches in twenty-four hours. We had tried to salvage the harvest, working with each bunch, picking away the mold on each grape. For a few days, the sun had appeared and the ground began to dry; we made a crude dehydrator to speed the process. Then another storm and another inch. Saying he couldn't stand the sight of the rot, Dad had hooked up the tractor and in a single day disked under the entire crop.

This time rain ended the next day. We walked outside, dodging the deeper puddles. I wanted to hope, to try and save something. Dad bent over a tray, picked up a bunch, and shook off the water. The skins of the grapes, half raisins by now, had already decayed into a yellowish brown. As Dad ran his hand over the bunch, the skins broke and the meat of the grapes oozed onto his finger.

He carefully replaced the bunch, rose, and said, "I'm not going to spend the next couple of months crawling around on my knees. Not for this crap." He turned toward the shed, grabbed his shovel, and left for a walk through his fields.

## Diary of a Raisin Harvest

LATE AUGUST.

Workers scarce and in demand. Harvest delayed. I may not be able to pick for weeks. From the porch I watch the grapes grow heavy. Some of the berries are turning amber; swollen with juice, they are ready to be picked. I rationalize that by delaying harvest, sugars can increase even more and each bunch will gain in weight. They estimate one point of Brix—a measure of sweetness—gained each week. Translation: about a 5 percent weight gain. Greed helps justify the delay in harvest.

I think about my Sun Crest peaches and their successful year. But on a farm, everything becomes connected and interwoven. Next year a good grape crop may be what I need in order to keep the peaches, a successful raisin harvest may allow for many more peach harvests in the future. Suddenly peaches and the late summer raisin weather are related more than ever. I can no longer ignore thoughts about September rains.

Without workers, I have little choice but to gamble and wait. Instead I'll watch the grapes growing fat. I explain my strategy to Dad. He nods. He understands how I feel about another uncontrolled force in this farming game. He consoles me by saying, "You never know, maybe we can count on the weather in September." We both know he is lying.

You can't trust the weather. Even during my few years of farming, I have witnessed four devastating years where thousands and thousands of trays lay vulnerable to the clouds marching in from the Pacific. As a child I remember watching my parents as they stared at the rain pounding their harvest and their dreams. Now I'm the adult with the unprotected harvest, my family and our dreams threatened.

SEPTEMBER 8TH.

Still waiting for workers, feeling helpless. I'm picking a few rows myself, anxious to have something to show for the last two weeks. I made the fatal mistake of selecting a long row. There's an unwritten custom in grape picking: once you start a row, you finish it, part of a stake you make on territory when you lay down those initial few trays from the first vines. The work, though, is cathartic. I sweat out some of my anxiety and tension and return home for breaks, too thirsty and dirty to worry about fields without workers. But the remedy is short-lived. Walking past unpicked grapes gnaws at my nerves, my stomach muscles tighten.

In the evenings I phone uncles, cousins, and neighbors. They all say the same: "Labor's tight and the picking slow." The usual workers who come from Mexico for the harvest have gone someplace else. Perhaps crops in the Northwest? Texas? We depend on labor from Mexico, part of a seasonal flow of men and families. Many come here for the summer, return to Mexico during the slow winter months, and return the following year. They're predominantly young men with the faces of boys. We're dependent on their strong backs and quick hands. And they are hungry for work.

Everyone is paying higher wages this season, but it doesn't matter, my grapes needed to be picked yesterday with no one scheduled to work tomorrow. Plus the grape crop is huge. Workers are detained at each farm for a few extra days to complete the picking. That delays the start of the next farm and then the next and the next. I'm a small-time operator with only about forty acres of raisins, so I'm last on the list according to the laws of real economics and pecking orders. Although I'll pay the same wages or even higher ones, work crews satisfy the larger places first, farms that give them more work throughout the year.

And I don't get angry enough. Unlike working with mother nature, where complaining won't stop a cold front or an invasion of worms, grumbling to a labor contractor might result in some workers for my fields. In fact, the louder I bitch the more pickers I may get. I talk with a neighbor about our plight. We both agree, if we yell and curse, perhaps we'll get a small work crew started. The old squeaky wheel theory. It's a game I have yet to learn.

SEPTEMBER IOTH.

Finally we start. A few workers arrive and the harvest begins. The chance of rain increases with each passing day. I feel more and more precarious. I can count on the weather shifting into a fall pattern, the temperature dropping each week. I watch the shadows lengthen as the sun continues its southern trek, drifting away from my farm. The nights are longer, sunrise a minute later, sunset a minute earlier. The change seems subtle but the grapes know the difference: they will dry more gradually with cooler days and chilly nights. I fear I may grow old this season.

SEPTEMBER I2TH.

I try not to get angry, although stress accompanies my morning coffee. I see an ugly side of human nature: neighbors competing for the same workers, desperate about getting their crop laid down. I hear stories of crews leaving fields half picked, lured by a neighboring farmer's promise of paying a few cents more.

One farmer uses the same labor contractor I employ. The contractor understands psychology well. He promises both of us workers, says what we want to hear, plays us off against each other with hints about more workers with more pay. I'm not sure who would end up with the extra wages, the workers or the contractor. Yesterday I had only one family picking my crop. Today a few other cars show up, with a promise of more. I stand with the labor contractor when the other farmer comes by. He pulls the contractor aside and they talk quietly. An hour later, the cars pull away.

This September, farmers drive down the road staring straight ahead, steering clear of a chance meeting with a competitor who was once a neighbor. Eyes avoid eyes, hands hesitate and refrain from waving. It's an ugly September.

SEPTEMBER 15TH.

On the news I hear that a weather front is approaching. It's still hundreds of miles off in the Pacific, churning in our direction, swinging toward the West Coast. No one knows for sure where it will hit. It could take a northern path and track toward Oregon or Washington, or swerve south and crash into warm southern air and break up into harmless overcast skies and tepid breezes—unless it taps into tropical moisture from a dissipating Mexican hurricane. Then it becomes a new monster laden with sheets of rain. Despite our sophisticated technology, no one can predict the weather more than a few moments into the future.

Old-timers understand weather better than I do. They have had years of practice interpreting the clouds on the horizon and the shifts of temperature. Their wisdom is manifested in a few phrases, accompanied by a subtle nod of the head or other body movement. My favorite is, "Don't worry, every wind has its own weather. You can't change that." A slight sigh and a gentle shrugging of the shoulders follows.

Part of me is beginning to understand such behavior but another part simply can't stand still and wait for disaster. I keep a vigil on the weather using all my tools: weather radios, updated reports, even radar imagery from Dad's satellite dish and the Weather Channel. Armed with my information, I can play weatherman and compare my forecasting with that of the professionals.

I detect two distinct personality types when it comes to predicting rain. One is based on a local TV weatherman named Sean who leans toward the pessimistic side. He forecasts the storm to move into central California with "possible rains of one to two tenths of an inch . . . a chance of some showers. . . ." As a private weatherman, it's better to predict rain and have it not come true than the opposite. The public rarely thinks of Sean during good weather.

On the other hand, Ron, with the U.S. Meteorological Service, has a different outlook. Farmers listen to his reports on little weather radios that play a continuous tape, repeating conditions over and over. Ron updates his forecast when needed and seems to use more precise language. It has to do with his audience, farmers who constantly battle the weather. I will make decisions based on his call: one tenth of an inch could possibly be tolerated, a quarter of an inch of rain requires action (like rolling trays to protect them from the moisture). Thousands of dollars could be spent because of the difference between one tenth and one quarter of an inch of rain. So if Ron thinks it will be light showers, no more than a tenth of an inch, he'll say so. On the other hand, Sean will give ranges. Both work under the pressure of being right.

Ron's forecast for the approaching storm sounds more opti-
mistic than Sean's. He even says the storm is tracking northerly
and the bulk of its strength should be absorbed by the northern
coast. The term *absorbed* lingers in my thoughts.

Who do I believe? Ron updates his reports as conditions
change. Sean projects into the future, the only reporter on the
evening news who has to predict the news. Weekends seem
especially difficult for Sean. He has to forecast days ahead,
knowing that once the Friday afternoon commute starts, the
weekend begins and most people won't listen to another
weather report. So Sean predicts "between a sprinkle and light
rain," hedging on carefully chosen words to keep his accuracy
rating up.

Ron predicts a 50 percent chance of rain. But he speaks in
terms of measurable rain (one hundredth of an inch is considered measurable), and I have to take that into consideration.

Sean uses language the general public understands. He says,
"There's a chance of some showers, certainly not a gully
washer, just something to help keep the dust down. But it
wouldn't hurt to pack an umbrella for the big football game on
Saturday evening." I interpret his report as nothing to get excited about.

SEPTEMBER 16TH.
We dodged a bullet. The storm passed to the north and we
only received a trace of moisture, just enough to keep Sean's
dust down. But there's talk of a second front forming,

What are my options? We've almost finished picking, and
35,000 trays of withering grapes lie on the ground, waiting for
the sun to dry them into raisins, the grapes still too green to roll
and protect from approaching rain. How do I ride out these
storms?

In front of my family I try to hide my emotions. I walk the
fields, visualizing the damage that may occur, imagining what

work is needed with a light rain, versus a heavy storm of over
half an inch.

Part of me tries to be objective and businesslike. With heavy
rain, I'll have to take decisive action. I'll need to take charge
and accept responsibility. But I can also feel a tightness in my
gut. I remain tense thinking of previous disasters, lost income,
wasted labor, and emotional turmoil.

My imagination runs wild. I feel persecuted by the power of
mother nature, who dwarfs my farm with her unpredictable
character. Yet I cling to a spirit of survival. I observe others, my
family and neighbors, as we brace for the storm with a hum-
bling humility.

SEPTEMBER 17TH.

Rain strikes the porch roof. I cringe and watch the yard turn
dark, colored by the falling drops. I curse the weather as my
stomach knots. Puddles grow and hopes are crushed.

Weathermen had predicted the storm would miss us or, at
worst, we'd receive less than a tenth of an inch. Yet the morning begins with clouds, high clouds, with some darker ones on
the horizon. I watch a satellite picture and it reveals an army of
clouds maneuvering off the coast, poised for an assault on the
beachhead. Something is not right.

The rain begins by afternoon. How it falls is as important as
how much falls. It rains in increments: sprinkles first, followed
by fat drops and steady showers for a half hour, then a pause,
an interlude before it repeats. I step out and check my rain
gauge. The first rains result in one-tenth of an inch. I sense
most farms in the area received similar amounts. The clouds
hang over the land like a thick quilt, a uniform gray that carries grief shared democratically.

A tropical storm is visiting our valley, a slow-moving,
lumbering monster heavy with moisture from the Pacific. As
it pushes north and east, the Sierras act like a mighty wall,

trapping our uninvited guest from the south. Clouds pile up against the mountains and jettison their cargo before passing over them.

I stand and watch. The potholes and divots in my yard quickly collect pools of water. Between the showers a balmy wind blows from the west. It hugs the earth, dries the surface, and soothes the nerves of a desperate farmer. I peek beneath a paper tray, relieved to discover dry soil; the moisture has not yet penetrated.

The storm teases us. A calm settles over the valley. I want to believe the storm has passed, the damage consummated. My emotions rise with the first rays of sunlight poking through the clouds. Then the assault strikes again and again.

The rains continue all through the afternoon: a light sprinkle and shower, wind, and more sprinkles. Evening turns into night, a blessing because I can no longer see the rain. The storm pauses, only to return as I lie in bed. I hear a tap-tap-tap on the roof. I cannot sleep although the sounds are soft and gentle.

At midnight the downpour begins. I stand on the porch in the darkness, the deluge pounding the land, tens of thousands of drops striking per second. I imagine the pools of water forming on trays and puddles filling footprints. The rain crashes to the earth, and I know mud is splashing onto the trays. Sand particles will become embedded in the raisins, trapped in their wrinkles.

I time the downpour with a watch, my own method to measure the rain. This episode lasts only a few minutes.

SEPTEMBER 18TH. EARLY MORNING.
At 2:00 A.M. the rain begins anew. I time it again but my strategy turns on me. The minutes pass and the gale continues. I grow to hate the clock; I want to smash its face. I turn on the

dishwasher as a distraction, and the familiar sound of splashing water fills the kitchen. It finishes before the rain does.

For a moment my anger is directed, focused, targeted. Then other emotions swell as the rain continues. I hide under the pillow, but the soft sounds persist. Nothing in my past has prepared me for this.

The danger of rain is part of my harvest rites. Yet each season new technology is introduced: bigger tractors, better disks, new chemicals and treatments; even with raisins they experiment with different paper trays and ripening agents to accelerate harvest. It's easy to begin believing you control nature. Allied with technology, who needs faith? Science does anything and everything, problems are solved with discoveries and breakthroughs. I am trained to be master of my land, to control and dominate its crops. Nature is gradually disconnected from my daily practices.

I awaken and discover that the rains have stopped. I begin thinking of the work that lies before me. I cannot fix the raisins. The damage is like death, irreversible. Resolution lies in living with the dead.

SEPTEMBER 18TH. DAYTIME.
We are tormented by a bright sunrise, the pools of water glisten in the morning rays. This weather tortures farmers with the promise of drying winds and warm sunshine. It seduces our faith and toys with our emotions, for we know yet another front sits off the coast gathering strength before heading inland.

We are taught a harsh lesson. Even though we can enlarge a grape berry by adding a growth hormone, kill a pest expeditiously with new chemicals, control a disease effectively with safer sprays, farming remains a sea of uncertainty. We have lost touch with more than just the elements. Our farms function

more and more as businesses with rigidly scheduled work cal-
endars. We trap ourselves in our offices, in self-imposed exile
from our fields. We model our operations on industries designed to produce a commodity. All the while we fool ourselves
into believing we are somehow insulated from nature.

By afternoon the other front arrives. Mold is already beginning to grow on the soaked bunches, their berries bulbous with
moisture. The rot begins to fill the air. I can smell it from the
porch. I search the horizon for blue sky but find only black
clouds.

I visit Dad and walk defiantly from the truck to his patio
despite the pouring rain. We watch in shared silence. Mom
sticks her head outside and snaps at us to get in before we catch
cold. She looks up at the gray sky and shakes her head.

The wind occasionally blows, darker clouds pass to the
north. There's little consolation in realizing that someplace else
they're receiving even more rain than here. The puddles creep
higher and higher in the fields. In some places the water level
rises so quickly and high, it covers the lower sections of the
trays. Berries float. It rains into the evening, shifting to a slow
but constant drizzle. The weather station reports that some
places were caught under a thunderhead and were hit with
over half an inch in a few minutes.

SEPTEMBER 19TH.
The rains depart. I restrain an impulse to rush out and try and
save the crop, and a voice within questions if I have the energy.
Oddly, I feel responsible for the disaster, not with guilt but
rather with ownership. Those are my grapes and my harvest
on my land. I am the farmer and work for myself, not for
someone else. I have to respond to this weather. Yet another
voice wonders if my fight against nature isn't frivolous.

Nature sets forth a situation, a series of unending events,
and we are asked to respond to them. Some affect us little, oth-

ers strike with such great force that we are compelled into action. We are challenged.

Of course I have the option to do nothing. Surrender seems logical, to accept the cruel reality of natural forces. But farmers think differently, like the old-timers who have weathered many a disaster with optimism and hope. They have the wisdom of experience and a tradition of care. I picture them tomorrow. They'll be out in their fields, walking their vineyards, sorting out the survivors tray by tray. They value their produce and the meaning of life that's so intimately tied to their work. That too is part of the nature of farming, the free and life-sustaining emotions of human nature. We learn to cohabit with our different natures.

As the final clouds of this front move out, I talk to nature. I hope for strong winds and warm sunshine. The wind blows and I ask it to blow more. I ask the sun to shine brighter. I feel much better, remembering that in myth and legend human beings often talk to nature. We lack modern myths in farming, trapped instead within a reliance on science to explain everything. I ask the clouds if they'll help by staying away for a while. They will try but can't promise anything.

SEPTEMBER 20TH.

The morning is humid. The sun is out and warms the ground and quickly dries the paper trays. Marcy convinces me to take the family out for breakfast, treat them to something special. She knows there is nothing to be done on the farm.

I realize how few people I've seen in the last few days. In town, people drive and shop and life continues as if nothing has happened. For a moment it seems like a bad dream.

SEPTEMBER 22ND.

I talk with city friends about the rain. Unknowingly they begin the conversation with a seemingly innocent question: "Does rain bother you?" Depending on my mood I vent my wrath upon them or unravel a tale of depression and grief.

I use different methods to describe the storms. First I talk about the acres of raisins out in the fields and realize a lot of people don't know how raisins are made. When I start to talk numbers they begin to understand, but saying you have 35,000 trays exposed only makes sense if the listener knows how big a raisin tray is. Some interrupt and ask if I use wooden trays. At least they can picture a vineyard.

Finally I translate the disaster into dollars. "I can easily lose seventy thousand dollars' worth of raisins." Eyebrows are raised, money is something they understand. Still, much is lost in translation. The farmer sees a lost harvest, the weeks of additional work, the salvaging of a crop. Dollars oversimplify the farmer's story and the delicate relationship we have with nature. Dollars ignore the power of emotions and tradition.

I grieve with a September rain, not from physical pain but from hurt inside.

I PARTICIPATE IN a legacy of working the land, harvesting a crop, then witnessing the power of nature to take it back. For raisin farmers, every September we reenact a ritual and participate in an annual rite of passage. Each season we age and grow older and perhaps wiser with experience. A few years of good weather have masked the basic anxiety of our profession, for we are always at the mercy of nature. This season she thrusts herself back into our work and homes and families. She speaks clearly and decisively.

If this were being told as a myth or legend, I would use the metaphor of a charging lion. I stand armed. Just as the lion leaps, I hurl my weapon and nothing happens. The lion remains suspended in flight; I stand motionless awaiting my fate. The moment is impregnated with life, not death, an instant that alters my life forever. Young farmers feel that moment of truth with these rains. I am scarred forever and can now claim to be a farmer.

SEPTEMBER 24TH.

As soon as the ground dries, we slip the trays by pulling each one a few inches left or right. We try to break the moisture seal between paper and wet earth where mold easily breeds. We also want to drain the pools of water where rain collects on the trays and decaying grapes float like drowning victims. It's painful to walk my vineyards.

I can smell the rot multiplying. Like a miniature factory, the fields breed spores. I become an applied microbiologist, monitoring the fungi as it spreads, regenerating each day, consuming berries and bunches. I learn about the three types of mold that attack raisins. Putrid mold grows like a white spiderweb, breeding where raisins stick together. If allowed to remain damp, it turns gray and slimy, the skin of the berry rotting like an open infected sore. Split mold cracks the skin, often originating where mildew flourished during the growing season. It often enters from the stem and works its way down the surface, ripping the raisin shell and exposing the internal meat. But nodular mold damages the most. It first appears slightly greenish and very sticky. With humid conditions, the mold can erupt and scatter throughout a field within days. It begins as a black dot but festers and spreads like a cancer, eating the flesh. As temperatures rise, the mold slows but remains entrenched in the raisin's skin.

Sand is also a raisin's enemy. Dirt particles cling to wet grapes and sticky mold. As berries dry, sand becomes embedded in their surface, trapped within their wrinkles. The grit will crunch between your teeth and vibrate through your mouth. It makes you cringe, like hearing fingernails on chalkboards.

For the rest of the season I will not eat my own raisins. Sometimes, out of habit, I catch myself gathering some loose berries and start picking off the stems, readying them for an in-the-field snack. But I stop myself. Not being able to eat my own harvest somehow symbolizes this year.

SEPTEMBER 25TH.

Some farmers saved their crop. They managed to pick early and had it rolled and boxed before the rains. I hear of one young farmer who said he was happy it rained. His raisins were safely stored in his shed, and the storms would help him make farm payments.

His story reflects how far we've strayed. We seem to have lost our sense of community, opting for profits first and a survival of the fittest. The rains affect the laws of supply and demand: the value of his raisins rises with each drop of water that falls on my raisins. He is a victorious hunter in the world of agribusiness.

The farmer who saved his raisins believes he armed himself with weapons of management, science, and technology. He confronted nature and beat her and now he will be rewarded in the marketplace. Or was he simply lucky? For one harvest season, he escapes the fragile and transient nature of farming. And in his gloating, he denies the fact we all live together and still share the same land, air, and water. His victory is hollow and fleeting: he may have won a battle against this September rain and will be rewarded with money, yet I know that sometime he will succumb in a war with nature, and in the meantime he forfeits the things that matter. I am a farmer and a good neighbor, not a hunter or warrior.

SEPTEMBER 30TH.

Even though the sky remains clear with a pale blue hue, I watch a storm brewing off the coast of southern California. Another tropical storm is breaking up into a tropical depression, which turns into an emotional depression for farmers. I watch a huge band of clouds break off and crush the southern coast, laden with moisture from the warm Pacific. The wave is pushed inland. Part of it splits to the east and heads toward Arizona and the high desert, but most of it tracks north. We sit in its path. I know this because I watch it all via Dad's satellite dish.

Initially this technology amazed me, this ability to monitor storms and directly witness their dark march inland. I sat in awe of the ability to recognize patterns, grasp the shifts in direction and chart flows. The satellite imagery is something to behold.

Yet even when surrounded by this technology, I can do nothing about the coming storm. I can watch my destiny, but I'm not sure I want to see it. Outside I hear the first rumble of lightning as the storm treads into the valley with a deep drumbeat.

I stand on the porch in an evening breeze, a warm, gentle wind from the south. I can see the advancing rain and know it will arrive by nightfall. I feel strangely calm, an odd combination of fatalism and numbness. My emotions were hammered all month. This final assault seems inevitable, even just and merciful. Is this how soldiers face battle and death?

The rain falls throughout the night, about a quarter of an inch; more falls to the west and to the east along the foothills. All night the lightning flashes and thunders around me. I do not sleep and spend hours outside watching from the porch. The rain comes in gentle waves with pauses between the showers. But I grow too weary to worry about the raisins. I finally slip into sleep.

OCTOBER AND NOVEMBER.
The raisins finally dry and we roll them without incident. An abnormal Indian summer strikes the valley, creating a miniature heat wave. I deliver the crop, and it fails for sand and

mold. I estimate that about 20 percent of the crop was lost in
the fields: berries and bunches stuck to the paper trays, ad-
hered by mold and rot and sugar that had washed off from the
tremendous rains. Raisin processing plants have a system called
reconditioning where they wash and clean failed raisins, hand-
sort and toss out mold and rot, then try to reclaim some of the
harvest. Some of my raisins are too damaged to be recondi-
tioned. They become distillery material for fermentation.
Some are salvaged, but I lose another 25 percent of the crop in
the process and have to pay for the washing and sorting. Farming finds yet another way to make money for someone else.

All of November is warm and dry, and we enter another
year of drought. The weather statistics are misleading, though.
Thanks to the September rains we are well ahead in moisture
for this time of year. I don't remember much about the fall and
do very little planning about the coming year. I know, though,
that after the fall and winter will come the spring.

IN THE DRY desert climate of this valley, the heat and sun scar
wood, especially the horizontal planks of our porch deck that
are exposed to the late-afternoon sunlight. I've seen other decks
weather quickly, causing them to splinter and embed slivers in
bare feet. Eventually those decks slip into disuse and emerge as
passageways for foot traffic, for shoes insulate and offer protection from the wood. The elements of time and weather change
the meaning of the porch.

The annual rite of sanding and resealing the porch symbolizes the end of a season. I work on our house and do not venture
out into the fields for days. I allow myself time to sort out the
harvest.

Years from now I may confuse the date and exact year, but
now I finally understand why old-timers can recall a particular
drought in the thirties or the storm of '48 or freeze of '72. Disas-

ters scar memories and tie people to a place. The bond can last a lifetime and generate stories for children and grandchildren. Buried in the drama are emotions and a wisdom of experience.

I now have the memory of September rains on my raisins this year, along with the elation of finding a home for my Sun Crest peaches. The two will be forever juxtaposed, as if in an eternal battle of compromise. They depict the harvest of a farmer, the lows tempered by the highs, a tragedy balanced by great moments of fulfillment.

*autumn chill*

# chapter eleven

# the year begins

## The Last Generation

Our old farmhouse has a young porch. Once it had a smaller, older porch, but it disappeared in a remodel in the 1950s, when the age of carpets and appliances raged and people took to the interiors of their homes. Status and comfort seemed to be equated with living "inside" and porches were considered relics of the past, like a team of horses or an outhouse. Somewhere in the fifties—with the newfound postwar American confidence and the invention of suburban tract homes, with the boom of babies and a new attitude of cleanliness, after a decade of Depression denial and wartime sacrifice—the outside was equated with being dirty, with its subliminal message of evil. Porches were lost in the process.

We added a porch to our old farmhouse only after I had been farming for ten years. It took that long before I understood what farmhouse porches were all about. I had aged enough to appreciate a shady resting place away from the baking heat of summer and a rest break that stretches from a minimum of half an hour to most of the afternoon, if I can justify it. It took ten years to learn how to look at the farm during the flush of spring growth and see more than grapes, prices per ton, and the hours of work that lay ahead. I now understand why an older generation sat for hours on their porches, watching the world go by between afternoon naps and evenings of quiet with the family. Porches create windows to the world and nurture a sense of place for a farm family.

Our porch symbolizes the blend of old and new. I spend hours with my family on our porch. My youngest believes it's a giant playpen, only we are inside with him. From my lookout I can survey the farm while smelling the aroma of dinner cooking inside. But instead of escaping from an open kitchen window as in the old days, the aroma of our dinner comes via a modern Jenn-Air downdraft fan, which vents the smell of a meal under the porch to the outside, teasing our appetites, spreading anticipation to all the barnyard creatures.

From my porch I witness the seasons. I watch the fog of winter linger in the vines and monitor the delicate pale green of new shoots in the spring. I can hear the flocks of birds descend on my peaches for a summer brunch and smell the aroma of the ripening fruit.

But out on my porch I enjoy autumn the most. The pressures of harvest are over, the expectations and realities reaped and stored. I look over the sea of vineyards to the peaches on the horizon. The grape leaves of spring have aged. With the first series of cool nights they turn yellow, then brown. They are tired. The peaches are ready to drop their leaves with the first good rainstorm of the new year.

On a fall evening I can feel the world change. The last generation of crickets sings and toads croak as they ready for winter's sleep. Sometimes I smell wood burning, a distant farmer clearing his land of unwanted fruit trees or vines. The faint smoke carries a whisper with it, of a peach variety no one bought, of consumers driving a fruit from the marketplace, of another farmer at the mercy of the public's taste.

During these evenings, I map plans for the coming year and changes I have to make, from pest control practices to budgeting and marketing. I hold my annual farm business meeting on the porch with an audience of two, the dog lying on his back on the lawn and the cat curling in and out of my ankles.

The porch provides middle ground, I'm half inside and half outside. I am out of the fields, away from the emotional attachment of ancient peach trees with their thick trunks, away from the gnarled and twisted vines that are the oldest living creatures in the area. Nor am I distracted by phone calls or computer screens or printouts of my fruit sales.

I'll spread out a pile of notes I took during the year: the scribbled thoughts I jotted down while on a tractor; the notes with the dark intense handwriting of stressful moments; the illegible thoughts scrawled during the middle of harvest. I keep a file jammed with these odd pieces of paper, backs of envelopes, corners of napkins, a note pad doodling with the genesis of an idea. All involve reminders about chores and needed repair work or ideas on how to better care for those old peach trees and gnarled vines. With the arrival of fall I allow my intimate feelings to surface. The day-to-day management decisions and their consequences have passed and I finally am able to give my suggestions and dreams a willing audience.

The porch is a place of transition, exposed and yet protected. From my shelter I watch the year coming to an end, the realities of one season merging with the hopes and dreams of the next. Out on the porch I reach out to a larger world; my private farm life connects with the public agenda. This is the season for assessing my crusade to keep my orchard of old peaches.

When I was a kid, many of us still had families intimately tied to the land. The migration to the cities had begun, but the majority of us still had family who farmed and memories of a place in the country. We could recall picking ripe apples and smelling freshly cut hay. We knew where milk, eggs, and home-grown vegetables came from and understood the meaning of the long hours of physical field work.

We understood the rhythms of farming. Spring meant work, summer meant harvest, fall a time for gratitude, and winter a pause for reflection. We were exposed to nature and witnessed the birth of seeds and animals, their eventual death from time and age, and how the cycle repeated each year. We visualized the fruits of hard labor and the true flavors of harvest. Many of us from this generation knew what produce was supposed to taste like and did not require advertising, promotions, or special interest groups to explain, label, and indoctrinate.

I had begun the year hoping most of us could still distinguish the difference between a green peach and a ripe one with real flavor, the kind that triggers memories of savory juices dripping down chins and nectar with the aroma of nature's bounty. I had faith in the power of family stories to convey the meaning of a summer peach.

For one final moment in our evolution as a nation we still have a community memory of the family farm. Many still carry the personal baggage from our rural past, a history of family members who sustained the land, and the legacy of a community that worked the earth for generations.

But this is the final generation holding an affinity with the American family farm. This is the generation that will control the destiny not only of my Sun Crest peaches but also of my way of life.

## The Year Begins

People often assume that the new farm year begins in the spring with the first warm spell and the stirring of life that breaks winter's chill. But veterans of the land recognize that a farm year ends in late summer, with the final harvest. Closure of the year is arbitrary; I often set a mental date, only to have nature and lingering warm temperatures stretch the calendar and extend the season for weeks.

A problem arises when seasons overlap with no clearly defined start or finish. I often don't realize when a new year commences until I discover myself well into the race. Much of the autumn is spent trying to finish one year while beginning the next.

So when does the old year end? In some years it's when I finally receive payment for my peaches. The reality of the year sinks in with the prices and numbers, no more over-optimistic guessing and projecting but rather a time to sit with records to determine if there were any profits. One year I never received a check and had a peculiar feeling about the just-completed harvest. It wasn't until December that I was finally contacted, the packing house hesitant about breaking the bad news that I owed them money.

Another sign of closure is when my raisins are safely under cover. Then I can focus on my jammed file marked FALL PROJECTS. The weather outside remains too good not to work. I hate to burn good sunlight.

For me, fall and a new year officially begin with the first cool spell that visits and breaks summer's monopoly of heat. In some years, the heat will return but I'll have tasted the start of a new season. With the first brisk northern winds and the turning colors of the leaves, a farmer's perspective changes. If it was a bad year, he starts thinking about the next. I know one fatalistic farmer who has mastered this art of self-defense and beginning anew. With the first sign of bad news, even with a problem in spring or early summer, he hangs his head and sighs, "Just wait till next year." (Perhaps he's also a devoted Chicago Cubs baseball fan.)

Once my new year began on Labor Day weekend. I had made only a few acres of raisins that season because grape juice prices were high, and we had harvested and crushed most of my grapes before September. The weather then oddly dropped into the mid-80s for weeks. I had just returned from a summer trip, yet during the entire vacation I was restless, as if my internal clock were set for peak performance. I felt I was supposed to be worrying about something instead of relaxing. I wanted to get started on new projects: equipment repair, new storage systems, painting the house, writing, playing with family. I started my new year because I had had enough vacation.

## Cruel Bulldozers

The new season starts when I call in the bulldozer to topple an orchard. It rumbles and advances across my fields. Veteran soldiers of trench warfare know this vibration, the shaking of the earth and the clatter of the metal treads as the creature marches over the terrain. Refugees from Southeast Asia who have settled in the valley to farm tell me it's the same with helicopters. The whooping and piercing wailing of the blades cause some to instinctively drop their hoes and grab their children to flee the fields for cover. Only with time and self-control do they stop running, but their thoughts and imaginations continue to race and create uncontrollable shivers.

I plan to terminate a peach orchard, not the Sun Crest block but a towering orchard of old Red Top peaches. These trees have aged and stand tired and worn. I tried to coax more years out of them and they responded wonderfully: this past year we had our largest crop in a decade. But I also saw something that was very disturbing. For the first time ever, my Red Tops were displaced in the marketplace by newer varieties, my peaches stood behind those with better color. Red Top ripens with a streaky red blush, while the new varieties are a solid red. A warning flag waves in my mind.

My problem began with slow demand, pallets of peaches unsold and sitting in cold storage, my fruit passed over for other varieties. I was forced to accept a lower price, a concession to the buyer, a compromised exchange.

My Red Tops were succumbing to forces beyond my control. I know this feeling from my Sun Crests. Yes, this year I learned how to find a niche in the marketplace for the Sun Crest. Could I repeat the performance next year for both varieties?

*Obsolete.* The word carries feelings of failure, rejection, loss. I can't help but take it personally, since my peaches embody my labor and commitment. Yet how can a food become obsolete? My businessman's muse answers, "Simple, when fewer and fewer buyers will pay for it."

I explain my dilemma to a friend and she does not understand. After an animated conversation I realize she is unable to think of the value of food beyond qualitative parameters. "Food is sacred and valued," she says. "You cannot put a price on your work. You need to keep those peaches for us all."

For a moment I bask in her flattery. I envision working my orchards to feed the world, my social responsibility, my contribution to the public. Quickly my muse responds, "There are easier ways to support causes."

I have other reasons for calling in the bulldozer that do not make me feel compromised. More than half my Red Top trees are over twenty-five years old, and every year I lose dozens of thick branches. They break under a heavy crop and crash to the earth in a jumbled heap of leaves, branches, and fruit. I've stood in the orchard and heard their shatter echoing through the field. When I turn to see the fallen giant, leaves are still shaking and staggering from the jolt, a cloud of dust enveloping the fallen warrior. I survey the loss but may not be able to pull the carcass away until after the harvest. The heavy wood is thick, lodged in the soft earth.

Unlike the Sun Crest trees, very few new young shoots grow in the lower parts of these Red Tops. The bark is hard and coarse, and new growth is confined to high sections of the tree where it cannot be trained. Also, most of the old trees have lost a major branch and stand lopsided like an inverted tripod with a missing leg.

Yet my decision to call in a bulldozer is complicated by the other half of the Red Top orchard. There, the trees are younger and by my standards still in their prime, less than twenty years old. (Twenty years doesn't sound like a lot for a tree, but most farmers consider orchards over twenty years old as unproductive. Considering competition and the proliferation of new varieties, growing fruit is now like horse racing: we compete for a frantic few years, then put an orchard out to pasture.)

I could keep half the orchard, which would complicate my work. I'd have to manage each half separately—irrigating, fertilizing, monitoring for pests—thus doubling my work for the same acreage. Dad's generation would have split the field, maximizing production and use of the land. He winces at the thought of pushing out such young trees. My generation wants to simplify operations. I think of the field as a single unit, with rising costs for the older trees. Am I lazy or am I rationalizing my decision as a type of euthanasia for old peaches?

The warning resounds through my fields like a disturbing whisper of a muse: *obsolete*. Battling to find a home for the Sun Crests requires energy and has taken its toll: I lack the will to fight on two fronts. Besides, I had a good year, with good production and adequate prices for the Red Tops, so I opt to end on a good note.

The bulldozer marches in to begin its task, and the new farm year begins in the 90-degree heat of early autumn. The massive machine rips and tears out trees. Branches crunch and crack against the roar of the engine. From a distance the machine works with a low growl, I can tell when it strikes a deep-rooted tree because the engine races and lets out a piercing moan. Over and over, tree after tree falls and is pushed into small stacks to be burned. A pillar of dust rises in the air like residue from a bomb. I can see it a mile away. The hot, still air traps the dust on the surface before it can gradually rise to the inversion layer, then the cooler temperature of the earth pushes the particles upward as the surrounding air heats and rises.

The stacks of trees resemble piles of dead, mangled bodies. In one day the work is done. The machine lumbers off, crawls onto the trailer with a heave, and comes to a stop as it nestles into position. I half expect a live sacrifice to be offered and consumed before the machine dozes, with a full belly, waiting for the next job.

The earth is left mangled: deep tracks etch the dirt, shattered bark and limbs are strewn across the field. Piles of peach trees dot the landscape, dust lingers in the air like fog hanging heavily over the killing fields. I'll let the piled trees dry, the green leaves wilt. Moisture will be sucked out by the sun, the wood curing in preparation for a cleansing fire. Before I burn the stacks, I'll pull a few thick branches and cut them for firewood, knowing they will warm my family in the cold of winter. They'll burn long and hot, the hardwood dense and heavy from decades of growth.

Paul, my good friend who's both farmer and artist, likes to paint these piles. He thinks of them like Monet's paintings of haystacks in a farmer's field. The piles embody more than dead limbs, they symbolize life and future harvests. When I stare at the peach piles, I remember certain good harvests along with the wealth the Red Top field brought. Once we hung a crop so heavy that every branch needed to be propped with wooden sticks. The sticks bent under the limbs' weight and looked like bows ready to be strung. Dad bought a forklift with that year's profits and often, when I use it, I think of that Red Top year. I can also recall seasons of disaster, the memory of leaving half a crop hanging on the trees because it would cost more to pick than the fruit would bring at market. The peaches grew soft and dropped to the ground, the nectar filled the air with peach perfume. I'd walk by and smell the peaches, hearing the plop of another peach dropping and smashing on the ground.

As the stacks burn, neighbors stop and comment: "See you've pushed them over." Then they ask, "What you gonna plant?" Even in early autumn they are thinking ahead, of re-planting and new varieties. In a pile of mangled dead trees, farmers still see new life.

### Indian Summers

We don't have a real fall in California, Indian summer takes care of that. Fields don't change into brilliant fall colors. Those who have experienced autumn in other places expect vivid colors. They may grow irritable about our ugly brown and the dry, withering leaves dropping from vines and trees one by one.

The air has grown dirtier and dustier from the months of field work and tractoring, as well as from all those summer bar-becues and the exhaust of thousands of cars and RVs that come through the valley carrying vacationers seeking to bond with nature in the Sierras. The mountains disappear behind what lo-cals call "smaze," a blend of smog and haze. It's hard to imagine that we live in a great valley. Everyone begins to lament how bad the air has become and recall how in their youth the view of the mountains was so much clearer. Each year the Sierras become more vivid in our memories.

Nature continually plays tricks on farmers with Indian summer. Once a team of noted long-range forecasters predicted an early fall rain on the raisin harvest. Farmers panicked as the coffee shop rumors spread. Many of us picked our grapes early that year—in August instead of September—in order to beat the rains. Then an unheard-of series of arctic storms blew in on Labor Day and stayed for two weekends, while 80 percent of the nation's raisin crop lay exposed on the ground.

A few farmers had missed the meteorologists' warning and picked their grapes extremely late, after the Labor Day storms. We laughed at their folly—no one picks grapes in late September for raisins. Then Indian summer arrived and the grapes dried a golden brown, fat with sugar and dark from the sunshine.

But Indian summers aren't predictable, and with any luck scattered rains will cleanse the air, settle the dust, and knock off leaves. It will feel like autumn for a few days, with crisp fresh mornings and the clear outline of a great mountain chain watching over us. Energy fills the air. A neighbor calls it true football weather. I think of it as the excitement of change.

Indian summer quickly returns to fool us. It tricks a farmer into a false rhythm, even though the calendar reads October or November. With such good weather there's no excuse not to work.

I start to fix equipment or begin an overdue repair job on the farmhouse. Other farmers will start pruning with leaves still on trees. My neighbor revs up the tractor for one more disking of his fields. It could be his final gesture to dress the land for winter, but I think it's the false attack of a spring rush to get back into the fields. We're all thinking the same thing: how to get a jump on next year's work.

Every year I begin a special project that will improve the farm, such as adding a new irrigation line, scraping a high spot in the field, or restaking an old vineyard section. I set an annual goal to better the land in some way, like the campers' oath to leave a site cleaner than they found it. Indian summers disrupt the scheme. Instead of contemplating the task and designing a thorough plan of work, I feel guilty about not being outside doing something physical. My work program suddenly acquires a design-as-you-go rhythm, a race to finish the job before winter arrives. But winter doesn't arrive with a snowfall that blankets the landscape and silences work. The lines between one season and another are blurred. I may miss the subtle differences, especially if I'm working faster than I need to.

The years of continual drought have almost killed me. These months are filled with monotonous days of clear skies. Each morning begins with a work list and the expectation that most of it can be accomplished. I don't have the weather as an excuse to slow down.

A good Indian summer can overwhelm you with guilt. Even the rewards from the Sun Crest peaches don't translate into confidence. I could feel cocky about the season but I think of myself as lucky more than anything else, for I have only won the first round.

*chapter twelve*

# autumn work

## Seeds of Change

My internal clock is set to changes in weather. Shorter days and cooler nights whisper a change in season. And seeds need to be planted.

I now realize that fall, not spring, is the best time to plant cover crops. The seeds can sprout in the still-warm earth of autumn, establish roots before winter's chill, and flourish in the first days of spring. This year I'll use a complex blend of seeds: common vetches, crimson clovers, and New Zealand clovers, combined with some medics and wildflowers. My formulations are not from prescribed recipes but are, rather, a random mixture that I create according to how I feel when I'm scooping the seeds from their individual bags and mixing them in the planter hopper. I feel like an oil painter mixing different combinations of colors to stroke on my farmland canvas. I will have to wait for months before I can see the results. I begin with only a mental image and a vision.

Some farmers question the value of cover crops. How much nitrogen do they produce? Do they consume huge volumes of water? What plants attract which beneficial insects? All valid questions that need research, these issues will take years to determine and may never be clear.

But the benefits of my fall planting go beyond making interesting plant mixtures and achieving proper nitrogen levels. Every fall I plant seeds of change for the next year. I am an explorer and adventurer, a wild man in the woods. No one can know the exact benefits of my cover crops; they are a blend of artistry and the wisdom of experience, a creation and reaffirmation of tradition.

And it is fun admitting that you don't know exactly what you're doing. This is the freedom of naïveté.

## Compost on Trial

Autumn is a season not only for reflection but also for judgment. Finally I have time to evaluate some of my farm experiments and plan for the coming year. One annual fall rite includes a review of my compost trials. (I apply my fertilizers in the fall because I have a break in my hectic work pace and the tree and vine roots can begin to store nutrients for next season.)

No good natural farm is complete without compost. Actually, only within the last few generations have farmers abandoned natural fertilizers for the ease and exactness of commercial ones. Before the sixties, most farmers in the valley relied on basic inputs to feed their soils, usually manure. In the autumn, farms regularly had piles of manure scattered around. The neighborhood filled with its odor. A common practice was to buy manure in the good years in order to build up the soil. I could identify which neighbor had a good year by the direction of the wind and the smell of profits being returned to the earth.

But commercial fertilizers became popular and farmers were won over with promises and initial results. Dad enjoyed the game of farming by numbers, believing in the magical power of 15-15-15 (a guaranteed ratio of N-P-K, nitrogen, phosphorus, and potassium), trusting the new sophistication of fertilizer formulations, and reducing soil to something that simply holds up plants. For a few years, these chemical fertilizers did increase production—the plants devoured their stimulants and their trunks and limbs bulged from their new ultra-diet. But gradually the soil faded, literally, from a dark, lush hue to a hoary light powder. The trees and vines seemed addicted to the fertilizer and grew rank and peculiar, as if the shoots raced to be the tallest and the plants ignored their fruits. Then I heard the gospel of compost and listened to the moral choices laid before me.

"Compost redeems the soil. Give back to the earth what was taken," I read in an alternative farming book. "Compost is nature's fertilizer, full of microorganisms that help build your soils. Compost renews the earth."

My dilemma is this: How do I weigh the spiritual virtues of nature's compost against the predictability of man-made fertilizer?

FARMERS CONSTANTLY EXPERIMENT. We try new products, new methods, new management styles, all within the domain of an ever-changing mother nature. Some call our attempts at research "farmer science," meaning it lacks the rigid procedure, methodology, and analysis of the scientific method. I resent the implied patronage, although it has merit. I have little scientific training and I know just enough to get me in trouble.

I devise my own experiment, using compost on one half of a peach orchard and commercial fertilizer on the other. My current longest-running test is with my Spring Lady peaches, those young, strapping trees planted eight years ago. I regard them as adolescents. For the first few years of their life there was no crop, then the next two years only a partial crop. I am anxious to boost production and settle my great soil fertility debate.

A year ago last fall I began my compost test, dividing the five acres in half: six rows enriched with compost, six rows with commercial fertilizer. I called a university researcher and he said my test plots were an awkward size, too large for detailed analysis and too small for a real farm test (most commercial orchards span ten-to-twenty-acre solid blocks). But I only had an audience of one, myself, to pass peer review, so I continued.

Next I found myself at a crucial juncture. I knew beforehand that rows 1 to 6 were slightly weaker than rows 7 to 12, with less foliage. At first I thought my study would be flawed and unreliable, since I had not begun with uniform samples. Then I realized the differences were small and a scientist probably wouldn't notice the variations. The weak trees worry me only because I'm the farmer.

But which half should get the compost and which the fertilizer? I flipped a coin and was happy to see that the strong half of the orchard would get the compost. I then questioned my lack of objectivity until I realized the trees probably would not be affected by my bias for compost. I applied three tons of compost per acre and on the other half used a mix of triple-15 commercial fertilizer. I later read that it may take years for compost to build up a soil. A quick one-year application might not have an immediate effect. I would need to replicate the experiment many times for it to have scientific validity. Yet I didn't know of one farm where anything was replicated exactly year after year. I was resigned to complete my trial, even if just because of a farmer's curiosity.

Spring arrived with bloom, fresh shoots, and blossoms—and work that should have been done yesterday. I raced to keep up with weeds and ahead of munching insects and worked myself into a frenzy. I didn't have time to worry about the things I couldn't see, and I soon forgot about my experiment.

Because Spring Lady peaches are harvested early, in late May, I don't have time for mistakes. With this peach I sprint from bloom to harvest. About a month before harvest I remembered my experiment and had to refer to my notes to recall which trees had gotten the compost. I couldn't tell the difference between the two halves. They looked the same.

Interest piqued, I began walking through the orchard surveying the foliage and fruit, looking for differences and patterns. The weak half still looked weaker but the fruit size appeared the same. The stronger half had darker leaves and denser growth; the fruit were perhaps a bit more plentiful mainly because there were more branches per tree.

I did notice some evidence of peach twig borers. Their homes are easy to see, because the tips of fresh green shoots hang limp and dangle from the worm's boring. We call them "strikes." Early fruit are not bothered by them, but the strikes in my Spring Lady peaches were like little red flags, warning me to monitor my other peaches carefully. I asked neighbors, and when they too checked their fields they found the same patterns of strikes. It would be a wormy year and we had all better be cautious. In my journal I noted that so far there was little evidence for or against compost.

I read a report that said different fertility programs induced different types of growth in trees and their fruit. Some fertilizers may cause rapid growth and push peaches to grow too quickly, making them more susceptible to diseases such as brown rot. I pictured such a piece of fruit like a balloon that's stretched so the skin is thinned and weakened. Another report hinted that too much rank vegetative grown may actually attract some pests, the abundant nitrogen may add a wonderful taste for the palate of worms. I walked my orchard and found no difference. The reports sounded intriguing, though, and that morning's walk was fun. I continued monitoring the field with a growing pessimism. In both test blocks, the trees looked barren of foliage and the peaches looked extremely small. My research created more questions and worry. My study was full of human emotion and drama.

In late May I picked the Spring Ladies when the fruit was blush red and the taste sweet. The peaches from the fertilizer side were slightly larger than those in the rest of the field, but the compost half produced more fruit.

I have never read the following question in a research report: "Is the cup half full or half empty?" Yet that was my finding for the compost-versus-fertilizer trial. Each block had different results, good and bad. Fortunately, not being a scientist, I will not have to defend my research conclusion, which is this: The success of compost or fertilizer at any given moment depends on your attitude.

I am happy the compost didn't fail. Next year I may repeat the experiment, but the virtue of using compost can never be measured. I already know one conclusion of the research, though: the best part of my study will remain the walks through my orchards.

## Burning Leaves

People associate autumn with the smell of leaves burning and smoke drifting lazily into a layer that hugs the earth. I think of a different type of leaf burn. I visualize seared shoots, burnt wood, and blistered bark.

I killed part of my peach trees in the spring by applying a foliar nutrient spray, but I had to wait until fall to determine the extent of the damage. My autumn leaves fell early, not from the first frosts but from dead branches.

It all started in early spring, when the first green leaves push open, their pale yet shiny green color announcing to the world the arrival of new life. For years a salesman had been trying to convince me to use a foliar feed, a spray of nutrients "to feed your hungry trees," and this year he was back. He claimed the leaves would absorb the mixture like a magical elixir and stir new life into my trees. I only wanted to help the weak ones, those that struggle to shake off winter.

"It's perfect for your operation," he advised, then leaned closer to me as if to share a secret with his chosen farmer. "Get an early jump on the season," he said, his eyebrows rising with the word *jump,* followed by a quick nodding of the head.

He painted a picture of peach trees like bears awakening from hibernation, hungry from their long winter sleep, rousing to life with the rumble of an empty stomach.

I had experimented with a kelp spray before, but this salesman urged me to try a new blend of micronutrients based on a unique formulation of fish emulsion. I should have listened to my own voice and its lame joke: "This sounds fishy." But with a salesman's skill he perfectly timed a loud laugh and I bought a fifty-pound sack because he liked my sense of humor.

I should have sensed something was wrong when my sprayer filters kept clogging with the mixture. I had to stop four times in order to wash them out, and the fifth time I was so angry I stomped inside to phone the salesman. He promised me a new bag and said I could keep the old one free of charge. Satisfied with my assertiveness, I returned to the fields and soon found myself trying to spray all my peaches with this concoction. Why? Because it was free.

Within days tiny holes appeared on most of my leaves, thousands of them per tree. They grew larger with each day, a pale band of burnt tissue ringing each hole. The pattern was distinctive:

every lower leaf from about waist high had this spotting, but higher in the tree the burn was less evident. It matched the range of my sprayer, which shoots out fifteen gallons of water per tree, coating the lower leaves but only misting the higher ones.

Two weeks later the singed leaves began to yellow. I phoned the salesman and told him, "You better get your butt out here today."

He arrived with his boss and at first hinted that I had a bad case of a fungus disease called shot hole. I pointed out that the fungus must only like lower leaves and how odd it was that it didn't affect the one row where I ran out of their foliar spray. Then they mentioned how the spray may have helped encourage shot-hole growth. I believed them for a while. Finally they admitted that a few other farmers had reported some problems but said they were changing the formulation process and I wouldn't be charged for any of the product. They brought out a bag of "new formula" and said I could keep it for next year. They drove off vowing to keep an eye on my peaches for me, and I never saw them again.

The leaves began dropping. On some branches only the tiny fruit was left, exposed without the normal surrounding leaf canopy. Dad stopped by and asked what was happening to the trees. I told him about the leaf feed spray. He shrugged and said, "The trees will come back."

The metaphor came to mind of a glass that's either half full or half empty. Spring is a time when the glass has to be half full because I begin the year without knowing the size of my crop, the quality, or the cost of production. Uncertainty comes with the territory. If I don't have the optimism of a half-full glass in spring, I can't make it through the rest of the year.

I thought I could trick my trees with a foliar feed, a feeble attempt to manipulate nature, to nudge her along. She responded in a way I could not predict, let alone control. The peaches apparently didn't like this fish spray and aborted leaves. However, new shoots were coming in to replace the burned growth, and the small fruit hung on nude limbs apparently undamaged. The glass remained half full.

It didn't take long for my imagination to take over. Wouldn't it be wild, I thought, if the fruit actually benefited from this defoliation and all the growth went into the peaches for the next few weeks? Or perhaps new, vibrant shoots would push from main scaffolds and make for excellent fruitwood in the following year? I felt a rising insecurity, though, as another voice whined, Half empty, half empty. The trees looked ugly, with a mat of fallen yellow leaves circling each one. I concluded that I really didn't know what I was doing. The admission somehow relieved my burden.

The foliage continued to drop and I wanted to correct my mistake but couldn't. I would be forced to wait out the season in order to determine how badly I had burned my peaches and if there was permanent damage. After one month of waiting, I hooked up a tractor with a small disk and turned in the leaves. I couldn't stand to see them on the ground. Fall colors don't belong on spring earth.

With the summer heat, my worst fears were realized: some of the dangling fruit began to yellow. At first, I hardly noticed the change on the tiny, green peaches. They were only about the size of a quarter. A few had adopted a lighter shade of green, bordering on yellow. After three days the trees aborted the weak fruit, the bodies collecting around each tree.

I rationalized that fallen fruit would only help the remaining peaches grow even bigger. Bigger usually meant better prices. I began to avoid the fields again, busying myself with the grapes, which suddenly demanded my attention. When Dad asked if I had seen the fallen fruit, I could no longer deny the loss. Within hours I disked in the evidence.

Still, I couldn't measure the extent of the damage. Despite the recent shoot growth, I hoped to see the trees flush with foliage. The yellowing leaves and fruit drop had stopped. Would there be a second round of defoliation with the next heat wave? My biggest concern lay with spotting of the remaining fruit. If the droplets of the foliar feed spray could burn holes in leaves, would each particle burn a tiny spot on the surface of each peach, a tiny spot that would grow and swell as the peach grew and matured? Spotting may not become evident until a few weeks before harvest.

I wanted the trees to tell me what was happening. Were they recovering from my spring assault? Why was I unable to decipher the extent of damage? I couldn't distinguish if the source of my frustration lay with my fear of the uncontrollable or the unknown.

I felt helpless, a parent with a sick infant. Despite all my efforts, I still witnessed more pain and hurt. Hugs help with my children—would they help my peaches? Over the next few weeks I added new meaning to the term *tree hugger,* which is usually reserved for a radical environmentalist.

Dad caught me out in the fields as I wandered from tree to tree, worrying about the upcoming harvest. He told me a story about June drop. In the past, it was common for trees to abort some of their crop with the first heat wave. One year all the growers experienced a June drop, with tons of fruit tumbling to the ground like hail from a thunderstorm. "Farmers grumbled and bitched all through summer and harvest and all the way to the bank," Dad explained. Nature took care of itself, aborted a potential oversupply of fruit, and produced a nice balance between supply and market demand. It was a good year.

I appreciated his story but realized that only my orchard had experienced this June drop and the peach market would not miss my fruit. I could identify with his reference about the grumbling and bitching, though. In spring farmers may see glasses half full, but by harvest they begin to look half empty.

Summer commenced with a ritual of pessimism. The temperature was either too hot or too cool; the crop was too heavy, stressing trees and vines, or so light that it was "hardly worth farming." Each cloud loomed darkly on the horizon. I constantly monitored my fields for damage until I found something, then proclaimed, "Why do I always find a problem on the very last tree?" At gatherings of farmers, conversations began with fish stories about the one that got away—who had the worst bird damage or water-stressed orchards or invasion of mysterious fungi.

I expected the worst because I live with uncontrolled risk, a self-defense compromise when working with nature. The cynicism helped remind me I am only human.

Over the next month, my peaches at times appeared fine, then a week later I would see potential disaster. I experienced wild mood swings, my emotions soaring with the scent of approaching harvest, then crashing with the sight of more withering fruit and dried branches. Even the day before harvest, scars from my spring spray were still evident: leaves with holes, seared shoots hardened into dead wood. Nature takes time to heal.

BY AUTUMN I can finally see the complete contour of the trees. Leaves begin to fall naturally and limbs become silhouetted against the pale blue sky. My orchard is exposed and naked. It has taken months for the trees to reveal the extent of their injuries. My foliar spray did indeed scorch many lower branches, but new growth has pushed from latent buds, a characteristic I notice in older varieties like Sun Crest. Many newer varieties don't seem to have this trait, the tree bark is smooth and uniform, and new shoots emerge from uniformly spaced buds. Old varieties like to twist and turn, with bud wood pushing from the gnarled burrs and pruning scars. They have an ability to rejuvenate themselves, regrowth emerging in the crotch of a cut branch or limb.

Fortunately my trees grew new shoots, the peaches did not have spotting, the harvest went smoothly, and I received good prices. I can relax now, the crisis resolved.

But being a good farmer, I find something new to worry about, thanks to Marcy's roses. A few years ago I tried a new method of weed control called "flaming." A dense patch of Bermuda grew beneath her roses, and rather than using an herbicide or a shovel I tried an alternative method, which uses heat to destroy weeds. I read that the surface tissue layers of most plants are extremely susceptible to heat, so a singe will destroy cells and kill plants.

I lit an old hand-held butane torch and broiled the Bermuda. The method worked, the grass sizzled and curled, but some of the dried weeds caught on fire. I immediately doused the dancing flames and looked around to see if Marcy had seen the miniature wildfire. The overhead roses appeared fine, but a week later their blackened stalks dropped their leaves. For the next two seasons, few roses grew. I had damaged the subsurface flowering cells and sterilized the plants.

Since my spring spray fiasco burned so many peach shoots, will they not bloom next year? I can now worry all winter. I share my concern with Marcy, inadvertently reminding her of the roseless roses. After my long discourse about the dangers of heat damage to next season's fruit buds, she says, curtly, "I suppose you'll just have to wait."

Seeking a sympathetic audience, I take Nikiko for a walk through the orchard. It's a brisk fall afternoon. I begin to show her the dead wood and try to teach her how to distinguish between a fruit bud and a leaf bud. She listens for a minute and then begins to run and skate across layers of leaves blanketing the orchard floor. Jake runs alongside her and I have to get out of their way.

Then it occurs to me that I may not know the extent of damage for years. Perhaps only the weakest limbs died this past summer. A year from now when I cut the dead scaffolds, I'll have new worries and concerns. I probably won't be able to determine whether they were damaged by the searing foliar spray or wood borers or old age.

Farming becomes a game of responding to nature. I will remove dead wood, knowing there will be more next year and the year after that. My collaboration with nature may be reduced simply to trying to get out of the way.

This I do know. The fallen leaves will become mulch, which I will eventually turn into the earth. I'll burn the dead limbs and use a scraper to spread the ashes throughout the fields. And an unused bag of fish foliar spray will sit in my shed as a reminder, every fall, of my burning leaves.

*chapter thirteen*

# orphaned

*Changing Landscapes*

When I left home for college, I sought to escape the provincial world of farmers, small towns, and country life. I longed for the excitement of the city, for the intensity that rural life lacked, for adventure beyond the horizon. I dreamed of exploring the city, living within a new culture and landscape, becoming part of the pulse of an urban jungle.

Yet some of my best times were driving home, leaving the city behind and slipping back into the valley. As city life faded and traffic thinned, I could see the faces of the other drivers relax. Then, around a bend in the highway, the rangelands of the valley would materialize, revealing a horizon of gentle rolling mounds. The land seemed eternal and permanent. I felt as if I had stepped back in time.

I took comfort in the stability of the valley. Driving through small farm communities, I imagined the founding families still rooted in their stately homes, generations working the same lands, neighbors remaining neighbors for generations. Small farms dominated the vista. I allowed familiar barn and farm-house landmarks to guide me.

Close to home, I often turned off the main highway and took different routes, reacquainting myself with farms and testing my memory. Friends lived in those houses. I had eaten meals and spent time there; I had worked on some of these farms, lending a hand during a peak harvest, helping a family friend for a day or two. The houses and lands looked the same, and I could picture the gentle faces and hear familiar voices as if little had been altered. As I eased into our driveway I'd revert to old ways, becoming a son once again, a child on the family farm.

My feelings were honest and real. But my eyes deceived me, tainted by my longing for a touchstone—a land where life stood still and my memories could be relived. When I left the farm for college, I could only return as a visitor to the valley, a traveler looking for home.

Now the farm is once again my true home. I live in that farmhouse and work the eternal lands. My world may seem un-changed to casual observers, but they are wrong. I now know this: if there's a constant on these farms, it's the constant of change.

The keen observer will recognize the differences. A farmer re-plants an orchard with a new variety of peaches. Drip irrigation is added to a block of old grapes, so I imagine the vineyard has a new owner—perhaps a younger farmer with many more years ahead to recover the costs—or the farm is now part of a larger operation with capital reserves to finance the improvement.

Occasionally the changes are clearly evident, like a FOR SALE sign. But I need to read the small print in order to discern if the seller is a bank that foreclosed on the farmer. Most of the changes contain two stories. One is the physical alteration of the farm, the other involves the people on that land, the human story behind the change.

I've been back on the farm for a decade and still haven't heard all the stories behind the changes around me. But once I add my stories to the landscape, I can call this place my home, a home that continues to evolve and change as I add more and more of my stories.

A poet returns to the valley and proclaims, "How closed-minded you all are." He comments about the lack of interest in the arts, in social and environmental issues, in the poverty and inequality of our life. "Little has changed in the valley."

He was born and raised here, which supposedly grants him license to criticize and lecture us. Yet he speaks for many who think they know the valley.

How differently would others think of us if they knew the stories of a raisin harvest in a wet year or a peach without a home?

## Risky Business

"Those who take risks are those who can afford to."

I wish I could take credit for this saying, but it belongs to anyone with the experience of making a living while raising a family. Farmers who try new methods, who change the way they farm, who can gamble to save a peach—we can experiment only because we can afford to. We are the elite.

I've become friends with a Hmong farmer from Southeast Asia. He and his family are political refugees of the Vietnam war. We convinced these peasant farmers to fight for the United States against the Vietnamese. Now we have an obligation to them. Vang Houa and his family have resettled in the Fresno area and are raising vegetables and strawberries.

Watching his family farm is like stepping back in time and seeing the ghosts of my immigrant grandparents grapple with a new land, a new language, and a new way of farming. Vang Houa's entire family works the land: children, grandparents, cousins, uncles, and aunts. Everyone has a job in the fields, weeding, irrigating, and harvesting. They have pooled their greatest single asset, their own labor.

Vang Houa's first-year strawberries are sweet but small and unmarketable according to today's standards. Later, a light spring rain almost destroys the crop when mold and rot march in. Vang Houa then discovers fertilizers and fungicides and how the established American farmers grow big berries and escape pest damage. He vows never to farm without some "protection" for his family.

I cannot blame him. His livelihood as well as that of his family and his extended family depends on the farm. Their dreams are built on those strawberries. I don't talk much with Vang Houa about my peaches and natural grasses and new farming practices. His future is too precious to gamble on good weather and riskier farming methods. Risk takes on new meaning when hunger and hope are factored in.

People sometimes wonder why farmers don't like change. After all, in today's economic system, those who take risks and make changes are the ones who tend to prosper. But a lot of farmers can remember the days when they were like the Hmong refugee. They still carry the burden of protecting family dreams on their shoulders.

I'm the product of a lineage of good farmers. I've inherited their success, which was anchored in hard work. I've been born into the gentry of the landed, a class of elitists who can afford to take risks like trying to save an unwanted peach. My status poses some ethical and political contradictions. Environmentalists may applaud my natural farming but they have trouble believing that some of the most innovative and risky alternative farming practices are being undertaken by some of the largest and wealthiest farmers.

Supporters of "environmentally friendly" agriculture encourage us farmers to talk with our neighbors and tell our story. What can I say to the Hmong refugee family if they lose both a strawberry crop and the ability to put food on the table? I refuse to become a missionary. I simply want to remain friends with my neighbors as we share common ground.

ORPHANED BY THE end of autumn—my numerous calls have not been returned, and I suspect there's a problem. Finally comes the answer about next season. "We will not be needing your peaches."

I am stunned. I was proud that my peaches had become organic baby food. I supported the product. I sponsored a fruit-tasting and passed out samples and shared my story about finding a home for my peaches. I even fed the baby food to my son.

Once again I will have to look for a market for naturally grown peaches with a wonderful taste. My Sun Crest peach is without a home.

I can respond in two ways. I can blame the nature of American business and its short-term, restless character. A baby food company buys too many peaches, changes a processing formulation, or consolidates and closes its West Coast operation. They try to console the farmers: "We'll be back in a year or two."

"But my peaches can't wait a year or two," I snap back.

Or I can go out and work in the fields. Such an option may not solve marketing problems or address fundamental issues about business, but it has therapeutic value: I can be productive.

Fortunately I have brush to shred. Even though leaves still cling to the branches, I decide to prune a few rows of my Sun Crests earlier than usual. I hire some workers looking for fill-in jobs. (Pruning the rest of my farm will wait until winter and a hard freeze.) Following a few days of pruning, tons of clippings from the trees lie in rows, ready to be chopped and shredded. Some of the wood is thick, the size of a finger or thumb.

My shredder is a violent machine. Metal flails swing on a rotating drum, smashing and splintering wood. The steel arms spin at hundreds of RPMs and strike the brush with the velocity of a gladiator's spiked ball. The cracking sounds echo over the fields. The tractor engine roars, the flails whine, and the clippings snap and shatter, splinters exploding out from under the machine. I wear a thick jacket but I can still feel chunks of wood bouncing off my back—and occasionally my head. Sometimes I glance back and test my reflexes as a blurred scrap of peach wood hurtles past my face.

Shredding is good work for frustrated farmers. A destructive child in us surfaces, and for some warped reason surveying the scattered remains of pruning brush feels satisfying. I finish the entire field in a record two hours.

It crosses my mind that I should market this brush-shredding work as therapy for overstressed managers, "a time share guaranteed to relieve anxiety." With the power of a revving machine under your control, frustration is released when the brush is mangled and crushed. Cold mornings could be perfect, the wood brittle, snapping with loud cracks that resonate over the fields like thunder. My advertising slogan could be "Tranquillity, let the wood chips fly."

But shredding orphaned peaches is evidence of a major flaw in my business plans. Having already pruned the trees and invested time and money, I'm committed to the coming year. We farmers have lousy business strategies; we start working and planning for the next year before we sit down and contract our crops. We raise produce on good faith that someone will want to buy it. We make the mistake of believing in the coming harvest.

Sometimes while shredding brush I wonder if there's not a better use for the wood. I've seen vine clippings advertised for barbecues, promising real country flavor as the special "aged vine-wood smoke curls around your steak." They get a couple of dollars for a small bundle of sticks, bound by twine. I could probably bring in millions of dollars with what I shred, providing there are enough barbecuers desperate for country flavor.

But I find comfort in returning the wood back to the soil, part of a natural cycle of farming. The woody fibers add organic matter, which quickly decays and becomes food for worms, microorganisms, and other wonderful creatures I can't see. It takes only a few months before there's no sign of them in the fields except the rich smell of earth.

Most farmers shred their pruned brush, although recently another option has been created. A new co-generation electricity-producing plant has opened nearby. Promoted as a recycler of agricultural waste products (like peach prunings and brush), the plant burns wood to produce electricity, which it sells at an extraordinarily high price. Power companies are mandated to buy this overpriced electricity because it supposedly comes from recycled materials and fosters a new renewable source for our power. It makes wonderful business sense. (In the last ten years, dozens of these plants were scheduled to be built in the valley but were rejected by the various communities. It's my feeling that they do not better the environment but, rather, deprive farmers of their shredding therapy!)

My shredding machine sometimes breaks. Belts snap, metal bars bend, flails freeze in place. I stop my work and fix the machine, it's part of my off-season work rhythm. Shredders I can fix, but the problem of homeless peaches is not so easily remedied.

I live and work with a paradox. On the one hand I no longer compete with nature in a game of winners and losers. For a year I have been working with nature on my farm, and I sense that something is beginning to work. A quiet voice whispers, "Natural forces are taking over and the land is beginning to take care of itself." Mine is a strategy of collaboration, not competition.

Yet I still seem to stumble, wondering if anyone wants to hear my stories, walk my fields, or taste my peaches. In the world of business, I need to look out for myself. If I don't win I could lose the farm. Maybe I need solutions that make good business sense, like building a co-generation plant.

I've spent the year building a home, a habitat, a place for my family and tens of thousands of other living creatures. The new farm year begins with pruning and brush shredding, returning wood back to the earth. It also starts with orphaned peaches. I have lived a wonderful year of discovery only to return to where I was a year ago, looking for a home for my produce. I again begin to imagine an epitaph for my peaches.

## Porch Spiders

Every morning I stand on the porch and peer over the landscape. I am overwhelmed by the rapid pace of change.

I monitor the grape leaves withering and dropping off the vines. The pace is slower than watching corn grow but the change is cumulative; each day you see more that was hidden. The green cover crops poke through the scattered leaves, the different seeds race to establish themselves before the first frosts. They claim territory and position themselves for survival. I have yet to decipher the meaning of wildflowers beating white clovers or the fact that crimson clovers bask in the remaining autumn sunlight while vetch seems to thrive in the dark shadows. I realize why they call it the *Old Farmer's Almanac:* when it comes to prognostications and predictions you have to have notched many autumns in order to interpret what you see on the farm.

With fewer leaves to hide them, I can see small animals scurrying as they prepare for winter. A quick jump and a rustling sound means a field mouse is at work, burrowing in the undergrowth, made anxious by the sudden openness of defoliated vines and trees.

On certain fall afternoons, the temperature warms enough for insects to fly their final dance before the cold kills them or their metabolism alters for overwintering. I can see swarms take to the air and hover around the remaining leaves, crowding together for a final gathering on the last cellulose in my fields. They seem to take flight for no apparent reason and partake in an aerial party, as if sensing the end is near.

I can see differences in cover-crop blends and uneven growth, certain rows of vines or trees shimmer with the dew, dense with new vigor shining in the morning sun. Rain collects in spots where I must have damaged the soil and compacted the earth. The mud and stagnant water remain for days, seeds drown in the puddles. I'm certain, though, that different microscopic fungi and mold now swim in the water. New life has been restored to my fields.

My list of autumn work projects grows long. Some of the jobs are repeated every year: repair of tractors and equipment, cutting dead wood from the fields, restaking a vineyard, replanting fallen trees. I am a novice with other projects and may spend hours talking with Dad as we devise a new weed-control strategy or cover-crop management plan.

I think of conversations with neighbors. Some are concerned about the loss of another pesticide, others complain about the expanding role of government. I can picture farmers shaking their heads over the inevitable changes in the marketplace and in regulations. We are unable to determine the direction of political winds and recognize that with each passing autumn, in more and more ways, someone else will be telling us how to farm. We no longer have much control over it. I realize we probably never did.

As the autumn ends on my porch, I watch spiders spin webs in the porch corners, between the rail posts, up at the intersection of the roof joists and the house. I sweep them away but by the next day they reappear, part of my porch, part of the farm. I tolerate them and only occasionally clear their webs when the dust has collected on their strands. The webs hang low, drooping with dirt particles, shaking in the breeze, empty of prey with the loss of their glue. I'll whisk them away knowing fresh ones will appear tomorrow.

*winter hope*

# chapter fourteen

# farming with ghosts

## Winter's Fog

On cold winter nights I step out onto our porch to check the thermometer. It has not changed much all day, ranging between a cold in the low thirties to a high in the mid-forties with a damp, biting fog blanketing the valley farmlands. From my porch I hear the *tap-tap-tap* of dewdrops trickling down the barren branches, falling and landing on the damp leaves below. I can feel the cold on my cheeks and the warmth of our home's wood stove still within my sweater.

Beyond me the vines and peach trees change seasons too. I think of the past year and the decisions I would have altered, modifications I can plan for in the coming season. Yet no matter what new course I may choose, a natural rhythm remains. I know the vines and trees will still be pruned soon, as they have been for generations.

The fog continues to roll in. Where it's heading I do not know. It passes in front of the porch like a shifting cloud. If I stare at it long enough, it seems that I start to move instead. I imagine our farmhouse cutting through the gray mist like a lost ship, my porch transformed into the bridge. I lean against the rail and peer into the drifting fog as my vessel heads into the night.

I sail on, the thermometer the only instrument on board. I like watching the gradual temperature changes, the measurement of a cold front moving in or the dramatic drop in readings with the loss of sunlight. Several years ago an arctic blast moved into the valley like a silent wolf. For days it hunted, freezing oranges and killing trees. I monitored its progress on my thermometer, recording historic low temperatures—dropping below twenty and never rising above freezing even in sunshine. Farmers could do little except watch. We only had our thermometers to help us verify what we already knew.

But a thermometer enables me to see the wild. The arctic wolf of that winter came alive in the dropping mercury. During the summer a different creature ventures into our valley—the searing heat that stays above 100 degrees into the evening hours. My senses feel the extremes and my thermometer enables me to process the impressions like a series of snapshots. The wild is seen.

A naturalist may disagree, claiming that agriculture tames the wild and farmers manipulate their world to disable the beast of nature. Judging by my last year trying to save a peach, though, I'd say that that gives us farmers too much credit. On a farm, much more is out of control than is in control. I fool myself when I call myself master of my farm. My thermometer reveals my impotence, for I cannot even consistently predict a day's highs or lows.

The fog carries a deep, penetrating cold with it. It doesn't take long before I'm chilled to the bone, especially when I'm in the fields, walking in the damp grass. Once my boots and pants get wet, I have only hours before my legs grow numb. At night while standing on my porch deck, I feel the fog invade my clothes, infiltrating the layers, announcing itself with my involuntary shiver.

I return inside, where I can watch the fog sail past our large windows. We have few curtains in our house, most of our windows are bare. From the inside I can see the panorama of the farm. I am exposed to the wild nature beyond the glass. I've spent hours in front of the windows, watching storms march in from the west and the wind blow rain and hail onto the porch. I can witness the sun rise and set on the mountains that ring the valley, study the ripples of August heat rising from the earth, and feel the glass warm against my skin.

The exchange is reciprocal, especially during the winter. The cold easily permeates the interiors, chilling the house and forcing me to wear sweaters even inside. The intrusion is welcomed, though, the seasons a natural cadence I feel within, a natural clock I respond to.

The change of season connects me with the surrounding wild, a wild I work within. I grow crops from the earth and have discovered that the best soil is also wild. This past year I have learned that productivity is little more than managed chaos, wildness the source of fertility.

In the fog I can hear the voices of farmers before me. Once I believed their old stubborn ways had no place in the progressive world of modern farming. But now they sing of traditions that have a place in my winter season more than ever.

Two wind socks flutter in the shifting fog. In Japanese, the wind is called *kami,* with an honorific *sama* often added. Wind is respected and revered, *kamisama* becomes a spirit that's alive. I can see that spirit in a wind sock, the energy captured for a moment in a dance of colors, then released as the tail flaps and waves.

Even in winter there is life on the farm. I feel something sacred, a meaning added to my work and my peaches and grapes. I feel connected with the universe. The world of nature and human nature are my teachers, showing and not telling me the secrets of the wild and sacred. From my porch deck I sail into a new world. Discoveries loom in the fog, opportunities inhabit this wilderness. It is a sacred place for myself and my family because I can call this farm home.

## Farming with Ghosts

Silently I stand in the fog. The wet cloud envelops my farm, I cannot see more than a hundred feet. A dense billow rolls past and the barn disappears from view. I can barely distinguish the outline of the vines across my driveway, their stumps and arms like a band of tiny people marching in the mist. Marcy and the children pile into the car for work and school and, like a spaceship rocketing into the clouds, the car also disappears into the gray. I strain to hear the engine roar and fade in the distance.

The fog beguiles my senses, my vision is restricted and unreliable. Sounds seem to carry long distances. Do noises really echo differently in fog? Or is it that, without sight, I rely on my other senses and literally hear more? The grayness acts as a filter. I can hear individual noises distinctly: a dog yelps, a truck roars along the road, voices speaking Spanish carry through the mist. I listen to laughter and some Mexican music.

The fog shifts, yet I cannot decipher its direction. I'm used to monitoring clouds, especially threatening thunderstorms. Peering into the sky I can lock onto a faster-moving, usually lower and darker billow, freezing the pattern in order to detect motion. For a moment the higher strata seem to move in an opposite direction. A trained eye corrects the illusion and recognizes that both are in flight, the lower layer racing faster, speeding along in a passing wind lane. But the motion of fog seems random, swirling and spinning.

By midmorning the sun emerges as a light gray sphere suspended in the sky. Some of the haze runs away from the heat and an opening is created as the fog seems to part in reverence. Quickly the gesture is reconsidered and the fog returns to block the sunlight, teasing us earthlings. The game may continue for days. Marcy reports that people in town grow moody; being deprived of sunlight wears at their emotions. They too are gray.

I find the fog strangely comforting. I work my fields with the mist dancing around me, happy to be alone and hidden. I can literally feel the silence, an emotion others may find in freshly fallen snow.

The fog is rich with moisture and drips from the tips of shoots and branches. I can feel the mist licking my face. On cold mornings the dew freezes and then melts with the gray midday sun. I can hear the frozen water come to life and tap dance on fallen leaves. As I walk the fields, my boots are quickly soaked from the moisture trapped in the cover crops. My pants brush against the higher grasses and absorb water like a sponge. I'll use the same route through the lush undergrowth and break a trail that will last into spring. Even into the summer I can detect the paths I've traveled before.

In the middle of fog season, my shears cut through branches as I renew the ancient act of pruning. It has required ten years to hone my pruning skills. After a decade I've gained enough experience to know how to prune and to learn what I must accept. With different strategies I can amend errors of the past by cutting more wood or redirecting shapes. Opportunity is born with each new year. This is where life begins.

And continues. In the fog I feel alone but share work with the ghosts of farmers before me. The primitive ritual of pruning recalls a time when the first farmers began manipulating nature. A sacred act is performed and represented every winter, a moment on a cusp of nature's timeline where a single act connects the past, affects the present, and determines the future. In the veil of fog I can hide or be hidden, a wet blanket embraces and protects my farm, and the ghosts are easier to see.

## Owls

They call in the night, deep voices outside my bedroom window echoing across the cold landscape. I can hear two, one in the distance answering the talkative one who sits atop a pole behind the house. At times their calls overlap and reverberate through the dormant fields.

Two owls return to my farm and announce their arrival with a nightly conference. I hope they will stay and join my farm. Despite the winter frosts, my fields are full of delicate and tasty creatures for their menu. Mice scamper over the barren fields. Small rabbits and gophers, confused by an occasional warm winter day, scramble out of their dens in search of food.

I've erected tall wooden poles for nightly owl perches. The staffs mark my rows but double as observation platforms for winged hunters. Nocturnal owls should have no trouble sharing them with the hawks of daylight.

Actually I need the owls. Mice, rabbits, and gophers run wild and multiply geometrically. Normally they are harmless, preferring the rich treasures of seeds and grasses to vines or trees. But I can see the nightmare of overpopulation. The stumps of a few trees bear scars of desperate creatures gnawing bark for food.

One mouse family invaded my irrigation pump. A small corner of the wire mesh was bent, opening the door for them. They must have felt cozy next to the core windings, especially on their first visit in the dead of winter when I had just tested the pump. The motor remained warm for hours and the mice moved in. Even though I didn't start the pump again until spring, the potential for warmth may have provided them enough justification for their relocation. When I first found the pump's housing full of their droppings, I immediately retested it. Mice nibble at wire coils as midnight snacks and can disable the largest farm pump. I was relieved to hear the engine whine and see water tumble from the outlet pipe. I straightened the mesh and cursed the damned mice for invading my property. Weren't they content with the eighty acres of winter grass covers I provided them?

Gophers create different problems. During my summer irrigations, their holes and tunnels change the course of my water, redirecting it from one row to another. I often play irrigation roulette, a game of chance to see which row will fill with water. For years my fields received free water from a neighbor when a family of gophers created a secret underground passage that connected his field with mine. Whenever he'd irrigate, my rows received his water too.

Lately I notice that the mice and gophers seem to be organizing, fighting back and reclaiming territory. They seem to be rising in numbers, not only in my fields but especially on farms that utilize a preemergent herbicide program. There, with a barren landscape, the mice have been driven out of their natural habitat in search of new homes. Sheds, barns, houses, and pumps have been invaded, desperate acts by desperate creatures.

Gophers, though, have a wicked streak of vengeance. Every year more and more farms are expanding into previously undeveloped territory such as virgin hillsides and uneven terrain. New technology accompanies the transformation, drip irrigation systems are commonplace, the black plastic hose lines stretch over miles and miles of new farmland. But the gophers of the world have united against this intrusion upon their sacred ground. They attack these new settlements, gnawing on the plastic hoses. This terrorist activity forces farmers to spend hours checking for severed lines and spurting water.

Farmers wage a campaign to purge these vertebrate pests. Fields are disked and no weed is left standing, a scorched-earth policy. (Poison may be set out, but farm dogs have a bad habit of getting confused and eating the bait. Eradication becomes very expensive with the addition of a veterinarian's stomach-pumping bill.) I know of one farmer who ends his winter by setting dozens of snares and checking them every morning. He reminds me more of a trapper than a farmer, spending hours on his early morning rounds. Most of his efforts are only minimally successful before a new population migrates to reconquer the territory.

Owls are wonderful hunters for gophers and mice. As a ten-year-old, I discovered a pile of small skulls and bones in a neighbor's old dairy barn. Three farm boys—my brother, a neighbor's son, and I—explored the wooden cavern. Sitting above the pile of bones in the dim light was an old barn owl. (Actually it was a great horned owl, but we had discovered it in the barn.)

We quietly backed outside and whispered to one another, the excitement making our voices crack. We talked about the bones, the owl's dark hiding place, and the size of the creature. I wanted to see the owl fly. Imagination and the thrill of discovery took control; we concluded that the best strategy was to shoot BBs at it to scare it into flight.

We returned to the shadows with our guns, then got into an argument over who would shoot first. My claim was that I'd seen the bones first, but my brother had spied the owl, and it was

the neighbor kid's barn. We opted for collaboration, agreeing to
shoot at the same time. We didn't think all three shots would hit
the target.

The owl was stunned by our aim. He staggered and tried to
fly, flapping his wings, churning straw and dust into the air. We
panicked, imagining the talons attacking us. We recocked our
guns and shot again and again. The owl could not take flight
and bounced against the barn walls and settled again on a rail
ledge. Explorers turned conquerors, we shot and shot until the
owl finally fell. Between the barn wood siding, streaks of sunlight penetrated the darkness and drew lines across his body.
Dust danced in the slits of the sunbeams. We abandoned the
carcass and took an oath to remain silent.

The next day at lunch, Dad talked about his gopher problem
and I told him about the pile of bones we had found. I wasn't
going to mention the owl, but then he asked where the bones
came from and I described the great bird. I tried to avoid any
conversation about our shooting, mentioning only that we'd
tried to scare it. Dad asked how, and I blurted "With BBs" before I could think. For days my brother was furious at me and
Dad was disappointed. He visited our neighbor to apologize,
but the neighbor already knew.

I regret the senseless killing. If I had known more, could I
have saved the owl? Should I have protected the owl and opted
for the rabbits that fed on tender vine and orchard plantings?
Could I have drawn a line between foolish killing and the sport
of hunting?

As a child, I recall asking my parents about hunting but
heard few answers. Instead, things like rabbit roundups linger in
my memory. Local farmers organized this annual Washington's
Birthday gathering, where the community would get together
for a hunt to protect vineyards and young orchards from hungry

rabbits. The roundup day began with a breakfast at the American Legion hall. Men with shotguns would drink coffee, visit, and enjoy the holiday. Then they'd walk to their stations, which were spaced about fifty feet apart along a road. At the signal (probably a gunshot) they'd march westward in a four- or five-mile-long line, loudly advancing, scaring rabbits out of their fields, shooting many along the way. A truck would follow and the dead rabbits would be tossed in, their bodies piled like trash.

I sometimes wonder: Had I farmed during the age of roundups, would I have protested the killing? Or would I have accepted these traditions and walked alongside a neighbor? An old-timer says he misses roundup days. During a conversation I sense that what he misses is having young people on our farms. Fewer and fewer shotguns are being passed down to the next generation of farm boys.

I WELCOME THE owls that come and call in the night. We can join forces as hunters. But where will my new owls live? The old red barn where owls once roosted was demolished ten years ago. It was built for hay and dairy cows, not for forklifts and peach bins. Also missing from the farm are the old thickets of willows and cottonwoods where owls could roost. Today we farm the entire landscape. I conclude I will need to do more than simply stop hunting owls, I will have to build them a home.

My owl box will be made from old raisin sweatboxes. No one uses sweatboxes anymore. They're from the generation of raisin farmers that predates forklifts. We have a few hundred boxes stacked around the shed, more of a weather break than anything else, but they're occasionally useful for odd jobs like carrying dead vines or broken cement valves. The boxes have aged, their wood now a dark gray from rain and dust. I try washing one, and my rag scrapes decades of dirt from the wood. No matter how long I work, the water only loosens another layer of dust. I sense owls will appreciate old sweatbox wood for their nests as opposed to clear, smooth green lumber from the mill. I believe they won't trust something new, which would appear more like a trap, too clean and unseasoned.

I'll construct a simple two-by-four-foot box, with an opening about twelve inches long and a layer of shavings lining the bottom. I plan first to nail it to my remaining wood barn, sister to the old hay and dairy barn we once had. Facing the east, protected from the summer afternoon sun, the owls can look out over a low vineyard. I'll be able to see the box from my front porch, hear the *hoo-hooooo-hoo-hoo* of the great horned owl, and sleep well knowing I have a guardian perched there, watching over my farm.

The owls may not like the location. It may be too close to the farmhouse, too close to our car engines and tractors. The ghost of the old great horned owl may warn them, and I'll have to wait another year and put my owl box someplace else in time for nesting. But my invitation will remain. The owls can't go home to old barns that are no longer here, nor can I rebuild the past. But we can both enjoy the pruned vines and trees and revel in the winter cover crops teeming with life.

## Farm Junk Piles

Most family farms have their own junk pile. Tucked behind the barn or out back near an outbuilding sits a gathering of old tools, machine parts, and remnants of discarded equipment. It lies hidden, obscured by the fog. Moisture paints the rusting metal a dark brown. These piles tell a story of memories and histories, of who you are and where you have been. This collection links generations of farmers to a piece of shared land.

In junk piles the past resides with the present. Scraps of sheet metal become patches on leaking raisin bins. A frozen drive chain from a retired spreader is split into dozens of pieces and lent to repair broken chains on other machines. A set of old pickup wheels and axles is borrowed from the pile and fashioned into the frame for a vineyard wagon. Our collection has an old, rusting hay baler we cannibalized for parts. A large pulley gear easily becomes a tractor weight that helps us gain traction in soft orchard dirt.

When I took over the junk collection from my father, the presence of an old hay machine prompted questions. Where did they grow hay on our land? How long was the field a pasture? Was it used for grazing dairy cows or other animals? Later I learned that my Sun Crest peaches now grow in that pasture. The lush trees and juicy fruit are well aware of this history. The manure has composted well within the earth, and the soil passes it on to my trees with vigor. My harvests are still part of the farm family before me. The old junk pile, shrouded by the mist, helps remind me of the historical landscape.

I visit my junk pile whenever things break. I often have to rely on the grape farmer's Band-Aid—of old vine trellis wire, a throwback to the age-old habit of fixing things with baling wire. There must be a phrase, "to baling-wire it," maybe originating in the Midwest amid the small farms of dairy cows, hay, and baling wire. Wire holds the hay together until feeding time, when the sage farmer will toss the three- and five-foot lengths of metal string into the junk pile until something needs repairing. The wire is perfect for quick fixes; it's pliable, simple to use, and offers the cheapest repair job available. If something breaks you can easily "baling-wire it" one more time, even over the old strands.

Once I witnessed its strength when a neighbor's teenager accidentally ran over an old wire pile in a pickup truck. The wire got tangled and wound itself tight around the axle. They had to call in a neighbor with a blowtorch to melt it off. I could hear the father yelling at the teenager a half mile away.

During the winter months, I have time to consider buying new equipment. First, I visit our old junk pile. Modern machines offer the excitement of possibility, sleek tools that promise efficiency and reduced labor bills. Just before the purchase, though, a visit to the junk pile helps me compare the claims of the new technology with the reality of the old. Junk piles are a history of what didn't work, a documentation of the names of companies no longer in business, along with a collection of each farmer's hopes and unmet expectations.

The purchase of new equipment creates opportunities, but a machine's potential is usually realized only with modification from my junk pile. Few pieces of equipment work as well in my fields as they did on the dealer's videotaped demonstration. I must make adjustments with odd parts, pulling something out of the junk and adding it to the modern implement. An old Bezzerides blade on my new hydraulic drag disk works wonderfully when attacking weeds. Together the two are a perfect blend of old and new.

My junk pile grows gradually, it is well seasoned. My part remains relatively small. I am still considered a young farmer and have taken more from the collection than I've added. Yet already I have contributed a bulky portable metal drum irrigation system. It is designed for someone younger than I, with stronger arms, who can reposition a barrel loaded with water. In my twenties, I had no problem with the weight, but today I'd be sore for days.

My father has a mental image of the pile as it looked during his reign on the farm. When we need a particular spring or metal shank he often recalls "seeing something" and heads toward the pile. He tests his vision by searching for a particular piece of old pipe or an unused furrow blade. So far he has passed each examination. I worry about what will happen on the day his memory becomes confused.

Dad's history is buried in the junk pile. The story of the farmer who worked this land before us is folded on the bottom, in stuff I cannot identify. I have no idea how many of the objects were actually used or what type of machinery they came from. They are from a different time and age. My layer is on top and includes roofing from the old barn I had torn down and bent metal grape stakes. The stakes will date my farming as the era when metal replaced wood for grape trellises. I also add a pallet of odd machine pieces, a collection of tool bar shanks, and some furrow blades from a good friend who no longer farms. His legacy joins my pile, our friendship renewed whenever his junk fits my needs.

A farmer's roots are exposed in his junk. The pile contributes to a sense of place about a farm that includes the people who are born there, grow up there, and work there. Over the years, I too have left my mark. As the pile swells, it records the time I farmed and lived on this piece of earth.

## Touchstones

People often venture back into the valley after an absence of many years. They may return for Thanksgiving or Christmas to visit family. They wander into little towns, amazed that the landscape looks the same, happy to see the mom-and-pop corner grocery store still open and the big oak growing. They rediscover old landmarks: the grammar school alma mater, the old cemetery, the dry irrigation ditch near where they once lived. They look for the familiar because they long for continuity, searching for a permanence lacking in the rest of their lives.

People don't want to see farms change. They drive through the countryside oblivious to the abandoned barns, modern vineyards, and new suburban tract developments with rustic names like Dancer Meadows or Sierra Vista. They enjoy meeting old family friends, who engage in long discourses about parents, grandparents, uncles, and aunts, followed by friendly orders to "come by" and ending with warm handshakes, hugs, or slaps on the back. I've seen travelers wink at their city-born spouses, grinning and whispering, "This could only happen in the valley." Visitors don't want to acknowledge change here because it would disrupt their sense of stability. This world at least is supposed to stay the same.

ONE NEIGHBOR WOULD often talk about the farm she grew up on in the Midwest. She has a knack for diverting talk about my grapes and peaches back to her family's small dairy, vegetable garden, and apple orchard.

My raisins would work themselves into discussions about her mother's holiday raisin cookies or raisin turkey stuffing for her Thanksgivings. My peaches connected with her stories about fruit preserves and winter pantries stocked with jams, jellies, and canned halves and wholes, along with pickled peaches and peach chutney. She skillfully shifted conversations into her memories of farmhouse basements, with details about the racks of hanging sausages and the bushels of potatoes and apples stored in the icy cold.

Then she often paused and a sharp sigh would escape from deep within. She'd shake her head and tell me how much has changed back on the farm. Her brother-in-law destroyed the old family farm, let it crumble and decay. She'd speak fondly of the old apple orchard, then frown as she described it today: the field abandoned, trees dying, and every year the apples shriveling and falling on the ground to rot.

At first I too resented the brother-in-law and his "attitude problem" (her phrase for his drinking). But during each conversation I asked questions. "Are there other siblings who could farm? Why did you leave home? When was the last time you were there?"

It took years before I realized that the farm she longed for was the farm of her childhood.

IN TRYING TO save my Sun Crest peaches, I discover that they are more than just food, they are part of a permanence, a continuity with the past. People who enjoy my peaches understand what juicy, sweet ones taste like. Biting into one may send them back to the orchards of their childhoods and that warm sense of constancy of family found in their memories. Individuals leave for the city, but the memories of farms stay behind to anchor personal family histories.

My peaches find a home with these folks, a touchstone to their past.

# winter work

## *Culling Old Friends*

A few of my Sun Crest trees are dying and need to be replaced. A year ago I convinced myself to keep them one more year, and I spent four seasons throwing both money and labor at them. But the trees are old. Removal will put both farmer and tree out of misery.

Old trees can fool me by looking remarkably well twice during the year. Once is in the spring, with fresh green growth and the promise of blossoms that perfume the field. Hope blooms abundantly in the air as I compliment myself for having faith in these trees. But as the season wanes, the fruit never grows and matures, the inspiring crop of peaches aborts, shriveled pits with wrinkled skin dangle on brittle, dried, naked branches.

In the autumn, when all the other trees have dropped their leaves, these old trees also look good. Their lifeless branches blend into the landscape and are harder to see. I slip easily into a quasi-religious fever in autumn, and a new year of faith begins. I think with conviction, perhaps my trees will snap out of their lethargy and rejoin us for the coming harvest. I plot my missionary work, nurturing and pruning out the weak growth, channeling the tree's energy to the remaining branches, adding extra compost and soaking roots with sweet pump water. I fail to compare the weak trees to the rest of the orchard, with their thick limbs and deep blanket of fallen leaves around each trunk.

But now the yellow plastic tape hanging from the frail trees I cannot ignore. I marked them during the heat of summer when the other trees stood heavy with peaches. I recall a group of my farm workers taking a break from peach picking. Next to a feeble and fruitless tree, they crowded around a small fire and makeshift grill to heat a tortilla lunch. I remember the joker who thanked me for raising this nice shade tree specially for them. We all laughed, and the next day I located my yellow marking tape and tagged the tree.

At a break in the winter rainstorms, I maneuver a tractor into the orchard. Dangling from the draw bar, a heavy chain rattles and announces my arrival—this is the day I'll uproot and remove the dying old trees. I wrap the chain around a tree trunk and mount the tractor, preparing for a battle between man and nature. The engine roars, the chain snaps taut, and with only a slight tug the tree gives way. It happens so quickly and easily, the top of the tree comes crashing down toward me. Luckily I had placed the tractor between two large branches, and the tree falls like a huge V, with me in the center.

Each old tree topples with a slight tug. I drag the carcasses out to the ditch bank where they will be burned. While pulling a fallen tree down the row, for a moment I feel like a hunter dragging the hunted. I imagine having a conversation with the other trees, parading one of their own, trying to scare them into production "or else." But the drive through the orchard is more like a funeral procession, the remaining trees honoring their dead with limbs stretched over us in a common salute. The fallen trees lived a full and productive life and are ready to be culled.

## Pruning

Early winter begins one of my favorite times on the farm. It has taken all of autumn to recover from the rigors of summer, especially the stress of that final sprint to market and the recurring nightmares of harvest disaster. I have a friend who also has night terrors. In one of his dreams an irrigation pump goes berserk and floods a field, and eventually the water breaks over a ledge and pours into a river, sucking his trees and topsoil into the gorge. We try to decipher the meaning of his imagery and conclude, "It must have been harvesttime."

By the first frosts, though, enough weeks have elapsed to distance me from wild imaginings. I can celebrate the beginning of another year while leaving one year behind with a sense of accomplishment.

My body becomes anxious for work. I find myself unable to sleep through the night, my legs restless for movement, my muscles hungry for activity. My mind relays messages to relax and enjoy the shorter days and long cold nights, but the rest of me is overwhelmed, antsy and restless to get out on the farm and do something. Dad claims that city folks don't get antsy, they become stressed. That's why they join health clubs or take up jogging. But that doesn't work for farmers. Farmers' physical activity has to be productive, like that of worker ants. Ants don't ever seem to relax and just lie in the sun, and neither does my dad.

My thoughts turn to the work of pruning. Ideally the first blasts of winter have left their mark and stripped the trees of leaves. But I've seen antsy farmers prune while lots of leaves still hang in the tree. The work is slow and it's hard to see. I delay my pruning because for me vision is crucial. The art of pruning involves seeing into the future.

I begin with a walk through the orchards looking for dead limbs that need to be removed. I carry a small chainsaw for this tree surgery and do the work myself because it's hard to find a worker who can see into the future. I call this work "shaping" the tree, cutting out main scaffolds fading with old age, disease, or assorted problems. They are thick and may constitute a full fourth of the tree.

I force myself to think in the long term and allow imagination to guide my cutting. I can easily spot the dead branches by their dried, dark, almost black wood. But it's hard to envision new growth and the new shape the tree will take two or three or four years from now. When I prune I have to keep that vision in mind. Otherwise I'll hesitate and grow timid and insecure, as I gaze down the just-worked row and see all the butchered trees and fallen limbs lying in the dirt.

With a sense of optimism, I can imagine new shoots filling the blank spaces, a newly regenerated tree replacing the old. With healthy, vigorous trees the process usually takes care of itself. In fact, in some cases nature acts as my guide. A young and robust shoot may already stretch upward to replace a dying elder. My job here is simply to take care of the dead and saw out the old. I just need to stay out of nature's way.

But it usually isn't that simple. New shoots require guidance, a gentle pull to bend them toward the open space, away from the center and their natural rigid growth straight upward. I have to see with next year's eyes. I visualize a young branch replacing the old, a new limb that will hang heavy with fruit. Some trees have no new wood to work with. I try to coax smaller, weaker shoots in the right general direction. This requires very good vision and the ability to imagine these small, scraggly limbs growing into strong scaffolds and, in two or three years, pushing out new, healthy wood to fill the vacated space.

I've worked on some trees for five or six years and still haven't found good wood. I'm tempted to give up on a few trees, the ones that stand half dead with little new growth. But I maintain an optimism that new growth will come and new shoots will appear.

The hardest decisions come when an old limb is dying but not quite dead. It may have borne a partial crop last summer and probably can carry a limited harvest next year. But it's dying and the question remains: When do I cut it out and make way for new growth? As I grow more experienced, I find it easier and easier to make that decision. There comes a time when you see the inevitable. The limb gave ripe, juicy peaches for years, but this past season was its last. Its time has come.

With each dead limb there's hope for new growth. That's why I enjoy this part of pruning: I'm always working with the future. I'm like a bonsai gardener with my peach trees, shaping each tree for the long term. When working with dying trees I feel one of the most important and strongest emotions a farmer has: a sense of hope.

ALL GOOD PRUNERS have their favorite old shears with wooden handles worn smooth and oiled naturally by working hands year after year. Armed with such a simple tool, each winter I'll contribute to the shape and future of my trees and vines.

My best pruning efforts seek order out of the rank growth while acknowledging the seeming disorder nature has left me.

Each tree will have branches I don't like. Some are too horizontal, with flat surfaces begging to be burned in the summer sun. Others may fork too close to a neighbor and will compete for sunlight. A few thick and vigorous shoots push straight upward from the main trunk, and I'll have to trust the weight of the fruit to pull and bend the branch down into a graceful, natural bow shape. A good pruning job forces me to acknowledge and live with the wild.

I SCHEDULE A pruning crew, but before they arrive I try to prune a few trees. I used to think my pruning would be a model for them, an instant bridge between my English and their Spanish. But one of the bolder workers would always ask "*¿Por qué?*" and point to one branch. Then he'd show me how he would have pruned it. In most cases the worker was right. These men have pruned more than I have; the old-timers have years of experience I could never match. So now we exchange a few comments, they nod, and then they disregard my model.

My pruning begins in the crisp winter air of early morning. I bundle up. I can see my breath as I walk out to the orchards. Even the wooden shear handles are cold to the touch. As the sun warms the air, I shed my clothes in layers, leaving a trail behind me, a day's pruning route tagged by jacket, wool cap, and sweater; finally, when the fog lifts, off comes the flannel shirt. After a few trees a familiar rhythm returns, a *clip-clip-clip* of the shears. My thoughts merge with each tree, the art of pruning returns.

For peaches, the essential element is in the spacing. I first learned this from my father. He described pruning as counting, leaving one or two or three hangers, the first-year growth that branches off the stem almost at right angles, per limb.

Later, I learned how to count these hangers for the whole tree. Each hanger holds a few fruits and each fruit variety performs best with a certain number of peaches. For example, my Sun Crests are strong and vigorous, and I wasn't overly concerned about their ability to grow large and make good-sized fruit. So if I expect over a thousand peaches per tree, and each hanger produces two to three fruits, I'll need to leave about 400 to 500 hangers per tree. But my Spring Ladies, which ripen in May, could never hold such a large crop. And so for them I plan about four hundred peaches per tree, only one or two fruits per shoot, which translates to 250 hangers.

I could simply count each hanger to get a total per tree. But there's a better way. I look for space between branches. This works best on clear blue-sky days. When I look up into a tree I should see a pattern: the Sun Crests should be dense with hangers, the blue sky partially blocked out, the open space limited. On any given branch, if I can see lots of blue space, there isn't enough wood left; too little blue space means too much wood. The best farmers and gardeners understand this. They may call it by different names and use different approaches but they share that same feeling when they prune. The best pruners in my fields do too. They may count the hangers per branch, but at a certain point intuition takes over. Besides, they don't have time for such a calculated and quantitative approach. With over a hundred trees per acre, farmers can't afford to allow too much time for pruning. On my small farm I spend tens of thousands of dollars annually on pruning alone. It's a huge expense with harvests still six to seven months away and many more bills arriving between now and then. The best pruners dance with their shears, slicing and cutting and snipping with a cadence. Their eyes guide their movements, building to a crescendo where enough space is opened between hangers and the pruning feels complete.

Dad once told me a story about the time he learned to prune trees as a young farmworker. A crew boss showed him the same technique we still use: chop away and open up spaces. When the five-minute lesson was completed, the crew boss wondered if anyone had questions. No one did.

"Doesn't anyone think this is a sloppy job?" he asked.

Again silence, although a few heads nodded.

The sage boss answered his own question. "Work fast and clean. You better learn to prune this way, or you're not going to make much money."

Part of pruning has nothing to do with the art of bonsai and everything to do with the business of farming.

I BEGIN PRUNING with the first frosts and end when the spring sap awakens plants from their dormancy. It may take months to prune my farm. I'll hire help, and together we'll work every tree and vine, lingering at each as if to revive an old acquaintance. I may recognize my pruning scars from seasons before, large cuts scoring the bark like initials carved in a tree trunk. I sense a permanence in these marks, as if my initials are etched there forever. But wood is not stone and the letters change as the tree ages, an acknowledgment of the passing of time. I return and discover the marks are different, yet they survive.

## Planting New Orchards

Grape and tree fruit farmers are deprived of an annual rite that many other farmers have: planting a new crop. I may plant cover crops every year, but it's not the same. Peaches are planted every fifteen to twenty years. Grapes are planted once in a lifetime.

Planting an orchard begins about the end of January and early February. I consider it winter work because the trees still lie dormant, the sap is not stirring, the buds have yet to swell.

The earth remains cold and damp from winter storms. A new peach orchard will be my first planting of the nineties. A new variety will replace the old Red Top orchard that was taken out last autumn.

I planted my last orchard eight years ago, the same year my daughter was born. I have watched them both grow, hoping both would bless the farm with their presence. My daughter has more than lived up to my expectations, but the peaches have performed only adequately. The trees are not quite as strong as they could be, the crop is often small, and the fruit size is mediocre.

I planted my last vineyard in 1980. It replaced a beautiful orchard of Le Grand nectarines that had the same qualities as my Sun Crests, wonderful taste but poor color, luscious fruit that no one wanted. I convinced Dad to give up and replant the field with grapes. That's when he first met Marcy, but then she was only a friend.

She was visiting the farm. We were falling in love and wanted to do everything together, including digging holes and planting vine rootstocks. She fell in love with the farm and loved the mountains surrounding us. The landscape brought back memories of her family's farm and goat dairy. She had been away from the dairy long enough to repress memories of the twice-a-day drudgery of dairy life, milking at 5 A.M. and again in the evening, seven days a week, every week of the year. Besides, I had induced her to come to my farm on a spectacular spring day, when the air was clear and the mountains visible for their once-a-year show.

She was dressed in boots and farm clothes, old jeans and a faded shirt, too good to throw out, too embarrassing to wear in public. She was working with mud on her hands and dirt in her hair when she noticed someone walking through the cleared field toward us.

"Is that your dad?" she asked.

I nodded and jammed another vine cutting into a small hole.

"I must look a mess," she whispered.

Then it occurred to me that this was their first meeting. I looked up and Dad was smiling. I was smiling, Marcy tried to smile. The introduction was cordial. I enjoyed the work break, and Marcy was good-natured about it all.

I didn't decide to marry Marcy at that exact moment, but I sensed we had participated in a grand tradition of family and farming. Surely many prior generations initiated a future spouse by planting a new crop. Surely many a bride was introduced to a future family and the farm at the same time. Did Dad break from tradition or did he return home to tell Mom, "Marcy looks like she'll make a good worker"?

THE ACTUAL DECISION to pull out my Red Top peaches came a few seasons ago with a series of discoveries. A week before harvest, I found a few trees with huge broken limbs. Until harvest was complete, I dreaded entering the orchard knowing I'd find another fallen giant, fruit smashed and scattered around its carcass like orphaned children.

Every year the upper third of these trees grew denser, gradually shading out the lower sections. Branches from eye level down died from lack of sunlight. Meanwhile the trees spread higher and higher, and the orchard began to feel like a rain forest. The majority of fruit clustered at the very top and burned easily in the summer heat, making it an easy target for flocks of roaming, hungry birds. Soon, workers had to use towering ladders, becoming high-wire acrobats to pick fruit suspended in the heavens.

The death knell for this orchard rang clearly when I fell off a ten-foot ladder stretching for some huge juicy peaches. I was balanced on the top rung of the ladder, one foot gingerly placed on a tree limb, while my fingers grabbed a skinny stem with lots of leaves. As I rose above the canopy, a rank green sea of leaves appeared, with occasional red peaches like the one I sought dotting the horizon. First I stretched for my prize, my fingers just grazing the fuzzy skin. Then I lunged at the dangling fruit, managing to brush one and knock it off the branch. I gasped and watched it tumble to the ground, the fruit was heavy with juice and sweetness and so ripe that the slightest tap freed it from the stem.

Next I swiped at the closest peach, grabbing it with my fingertips as I felt the ladder slip from my toes. With one hand I caught a branch and swung like Tarzan of the peach orchards. It was fun for a brief moment, until I heard a snap. Half the tree and I tumbled to the ground.

I survived with only facial scratches and a nasty gouge on my forearm, but I still held onto the peach. It was soft and dead ripe. I turned it over to taste my reward, only to find that birds had beaten me to it weeks before. What was left was oozing brown rot. Treetop fruit proved very costly.

To the general public, farmers may appear stoic, with a strong streak of common sense and level-headed patience. In truth, emotions often are the catalyst for change. Crucial farm decisions, like pushing out an orchard, are made in the heat of the moment.

It's expensive to plant a new orchard. Each tree costs four to five dollars, plus the labor of planting and caring for it until it bears fruit. After clearing the field and burning the stumps and branches, I have to level and smooth the ripped earth. I'll probably spend a thousand dollars an acre over the course of three years before I see a single peach.

Beyond the economic issues, a new orchard clarifies values. I have to select a peach variety, map out the orchard, and accept the reality that I'll live with these decisions for years. A new planting is like having another child, requiring patience and sacrifice and a resounding optimism for the future.

When Dad started farming, there were only a few peach varieties available. Today I have dozens to select from. Some ripen in early May, others in October; some are full red, others a blush color; one variety bears well in heavy clay soils, another in lighter sandy ground. Few of the older varieties like Sun Crest have survived. The new ones are like thoroughbred racehorses, bred for a specific characteristic and trait. New peaches sprint to become the dominant variety in the marketplace sweepstakes. Nurseries race to be the first out with a newer, supposedly superior variety.

These new breeds come with little history. Rarely do I know of anyone who has worked with them for more than a year or two. When a nursery salesman suggests I take a look at a new variety, he means a quick drive-by inspection from the cab of a pickup to judge the tree without talking with the farmer.

One newer variety ripens about the same time as Sun Crest. It has excellent characteristics and good taste, and I think it will like the ground where I'm planting it. Also, I work well with these midsummer varieties that ripen in June and July, because late in the summer my organic farm is confronted by new pressures. Worms hatch and scour the fields for food, pathogens multiply and invade ripening fruit, weeds take root and go to seed. Also, by August my family is hounding me to take a break from summer work, a quick escape before the grapes ripen.

A small family farm can't absorb many mistakes and losses. I may well be gambling with my children's college education with this new orchard. I select a variety because I think it fits my farm, and then all I can do is hope for the best.

After variety selection, I'm preoccupied by the design of the field and the exact distance between the rows of trees, a space I can't change once I plant. Over the years I have collected a file full of notes, a suggestion box to myself about orchard replanting. Some reminders I vividly remember, such as allowing for more room at one end of the field in order to turn my tractor and bin trailer. A twisted tree marks the spot when I learned too late that a trailer and our big tractor can't make the bend without hitting something.

One note reminds me of the time a worker ran over a cement irrigation valve because it was hidden by a tree. Another note diagrams a six-inch strip of weeds that escapes our disk and requires an extra pass on the tractor. When I was starting to farm, I didn't mind the extra work; now I hate the additional two hours it takes—on a hot tractor in the middle of summer—to turn a narrow band of weeds. Years from now, when my children start to help and work the tractor, they'll thank me for narrowing the new orchard. An extra two hours can be an eternity to an adolescent child.

With years of suggestions incorporated into a plan, I can map out the new orchard. But while a design may work fine on paper, it's not until I'm out in the field that I can visualize the mature orchard. I jam sticks into the ground and imagine ten-year-old trees. I pretend to drive a tractor while pulling a disk, checking to see if the wheels will clear the branches and if the disk will have enough room to turn. I use stakes to mark one border of the field and then let them stand for a few weeks. I want to live with them awhile before embracing a specific plan.

A friend drops by and asks why I waste so much space in the avenue separating my farm from my neighbor's. He suggests I plant closer to the property line and fit in another row of sixteen trees. But I explain that an extra row might crowd my neighbor, who often uses large equipment. I can imagine his frustration swelling as my trees grow and expand into our shared border. Good neighbors are worth more than an extra sixteen trees.

I hire a trained work crew to help plant the trees. Were it only a few hundred trees, Dad and I could probably handle the work. But my new orchard will have over five hundred trees. I negotiate with the workers to come early in the planting season, before other farmers demand help in planting their twenty-acre blocks and thousands of trees.

My crew will plant the bare-root trees by hand, which is rare these days. Most other orchards are planted with machines that measure, rip open planting holes, and seal them, requiring human assistance only to drop the tree into the trench at the proper time. Instead, my field will be filled with a dozen men running after a stretched tape measure, marking the proper spacing with straws, then hand-digging small holes for the trees.

Roots are trimmed, leaving only a few strong tap roots, then jammed into the narrow holes. We lean the tree slightly to the north, anticipating vigorous growth toward the sunny southern exposure. Holes are filled, and loose earth packed down by boots.

The culmination of years of decisions is completed within a few hours. An empty field is transformed. I anticipate that with the first signs of spring, earthworms will tickle these new roots and the trees will discover their new home. They will push down and explore my land. I hope they'll take hold with few rejections.

A planted field exposes my opinions like an open ballot to the world. I reveal a commitment to my neighbors and those who pass: by planting a permanent crop I announce my plans to be here for a while.

# chapter sixteen

# return of the egret

## New Year's Day

Every New Year's Day we follow Japanese tradition and open our house to family, friends, and neighbors. Guests begin to arrive by late morning, and the first plates are loaded with sushi, teriyaki chicken, tempura vegetables, and shrimp. We toast with sake and talk about the year past and the year to begin.

Decades ago, I can recall my relatives and Japanese American family friends having their own New Year's Day open houses. I'd make the rounds, first stopping at a favorite aunt and uncle's place for lunch, a Japanese neighbor's for an afternoon snack, and still another aunt's for dinner. Once I became a teenager, trying to coordinate a quick visit to the homes of friends and a few potential girlfriends, the schedule became more complicated. But over the years, New Year's Day gatherings have changed. Fewer and fewer families host their own. Instead, they thank us and contribute some food to ours.

Most of the food is prepared by Marcy, my mom, and my sister, with Nikiko helping. A few aunts arrive with platters of sushi or *manju,* red bean pastries. As they hand me their dishes, they whisper, "It's really nothing. Happy New Year." They help begin the year with humility.

No matter how well Marcy prepares Japanese food, throughout the day a series of accolades will be heard: "What a good cook you must be!" I sometimes voice their unspoken words, "for someone not Japanese," and catch them nodding their heads in agreement.

Guests continue to arrive throughout the day. They first gather at the dining table, then move to a couch or patch of sunlight on the porch for more conversation as another wave of friends arrive. Attendance varies from year to year, depending on the weather or the extent of New Year's Eve partying. Just counting the relatives and neighbors, we'll always have at least fifty guests, and in some years our home has welcomed over a hundred. The pace is relaxed. We have grown accustomed to certain friends arriving at noon, others arrive later in the day and stay until evening, and some will join us with the evening fog.

New Year's Day remains a celebration. Food trays are emptied and refilled, children run and play outside no matter the weather, voices fill our home and farm with life.

We renew friendships as we cluster around the table and talk over food. Groups form and chat; relatives gossip and whisper; bows, embraces, and smiles are plentiful. At a certain point the noise level rises and reverberates throughout our wooden house, I find myself shouting with frequent toasts of sake. As the day unfolds, our windows fog from the moisture of intense conversation and serious discussion.

Inevitably, farmer friends gather outside on the porch. Two or three will adopt their roadside stance, a relaxed posture with hands in their pockets, or lean against the porch railing as if it were the side of a pickup. One may begin to paw nervously with his foot, making imaginary patterns on the wood flooring. Talk of prices and politics will blend with personal stories of success or failure. Enough time has passed so the mistakes can be laughed at, enough distancing has occurred so that emotions have calmed. The farmers can talk in terms of the coming year and the lessons gained from the past.

Some can't help themselves and walk out into the fields. An instant farm tour is organized with half a dozen farmers tramping through the cold damp fields. Most of us stroll with a drink in hand, others balance sushi on napkins. The parade returns to wives, who ask, "Where have you been?"

We then stomp off the moisture soaking our shoes and answer, "Any more food left?" The hike will have stirred appetites, and another feasting begins.

I celebrate the renewal of spirit on New Year's, a confirmation of farming one more year. I tell others, "What better way to begin a year than with a gathering of family and friends?"

I began the year hoping to save my Sun Crest peaches, now I begin the cycle of a new year in fellowship with others.

## Homebound

There's a Chinese proverb that says, "A journey begins with the first step." But it never explains when the journey ends. As the new year begins, I realize that what I seek is the satisfaction of growing my peaches the best I can. I relish the fact that people enjoy the taste of my fruit. Perhaps that's where the journey ends and another begins. My peaches are my gift, and with each new year the joy of giving is renewed.

My quest to find a home for my peaches began with farming them a different way. During spring I competed with nature, fighting a war with the weather and pests. My strategy changed in the summer, when I accepted the fact that I will win sometimes and lose other times. The key to farming seemed to be one of compromise, and I accepted this only grudgingly. Then a simple September rain forced me to acknowledge that nature will always, in the end, dictate my work rhythms. In the autumn and winter I farm in a cooperative, collaborative relationship with nature.

I feel like many of the old farmers who don't know when or how to retire. They're not good at endings and will probably die on their farms. My destiny is to work the land and leave behind a farm. Growing Sun Crest peaches is all part of my lifelong journey. Now I know why old farmers keep hanging on. They greet each season anew and maintain a passion for their work. They rise early, anxious to start each day. They understand it's the journey that's important, not the end.

A seventy-five-year-old Nisei farmer explains, "Farmers, we're like that Japanese character *hito,* which means person." He pauses, then draws a kanji in the air with his finger. "You know *hito,* written in two strokes. A long one with the other holdin' it up."

His hand mimics a long even brush stroke, a diagonal line starting at the upper right-hand side and dropping down and to the left. Then a short stroke follows, a quick flick of the wrist and forearm creating another line that begins at the belly of the first one and drops at a right angle. He repeats his motions, and the image seems suspended in the air: a long flowing line with a slight curve, and a second movement that seems to prop up the first stroke.

He continues, "A farmer can't stand alone, has to lean against someone. Today, that's the way it is."

My Sun Crests help me understand what this old farmer knows. I began the year ready to wage a foolish war, one farmer battling nature, my peaches fighting for a niche in the marketplace. Over and over, though, my struggles were resolved only when I included my family and neighbors as part of the solution. The greatest lesson I glean from my fields is that I cannot farm alone.

When I gaze over my farm I imagine Baachan or Dad walking through the fields. They seemed content, at home on this land. My Sun Crest peaches are now part of the history of this place I too call home. I understand where I am because I know where I came from. I am homebound, forever linked to a piece of earth and the living creatures that reside here. What others may find confining, I find comforting: I feel secure.

A neighbor in his forties insists that only the bottom line counts. He says he's not here to raise pretty fields and he won't farm for very long if he can't make a profit. I know that pretty fields are very much part of my annual profits. Farming provides me with meaningful work, a way of life that integrates family, community, and tradition.

Can I afford to keep my Sun Crest? Or should the real question be, Why not? My peaches offer me a taste for life; they teach me about the flavors of nature. I decide to keep them for one more season. I feel an obligation to try because I have the opportunity. The ghosts who dance in the winter fog whisper this to me. They trick me into pruning one tree and then another and another. They coax me into replanting a new tree to replace one that dies. They understand the power of watching a new generation grow and become established, the young and the old all part of a whole field.

The challenge stirs my emotions. I hope to leave my mark on this landscape like worn initials carved in a tree. I do not need to compete with others. I seek no compromises from nature. In the solitude of the fog I work with myself and my family and friends. I commit to another year and the decision warms me. I am confident new stories will fill my fields with life for the coming season.

### Return of the Egret

In the winter I often walk under a bridge where irrigation water flows during the summer. Along the sides are hundreds of swallow nests, tucked up in the corners, layered one upon the other. Each dab of mud hangs intact, cemented to the others by gifted crafters and engineers. I feel like an explorer visiting abandoned villages of the true natives of this land.

Every spring the swallows return to this ditch, my own Capistrano in the San Joaquin Valley. But this is a man-made river, an irrigation canal that brings life to a desert. The bridge is not a quaint wooden crossing; its gray cement supports rise out of the sand at right angles, an asphalt roadway crosses overhead.

The swallows build their homes in the summer, but even in winter I can picture them swooping and darting past me. As I stand on the bridge, they zoom beneath me, skimming the water. I like to imagine their view of the world as they launch themselves under the bridge and then break out of the darkness on the other side, flinging themselves into the daylight. I can see a burst of sunlight greeting them and a pale blue sky rising above the cool mountain water, green farmlands stretching as far as the eye can see.

This is the place we both call home.

A white egret comes to my ditch bank each winter. I believe it's an egret. I also believe it to be a spirit that comes to haunt the farm, and I hope it's the goddess of life returning to watch over me.

Years ago my cousin and I shot an egret. We were young, he was from Los Angeles, a city kid let loose in the countryside. On our farm, he wanted to live out his cowboy dreams from *Bonanza* and other TV shows from the late fifties.

We were walking on the ditch bank when we discovered a wonderful white creature perched still, stalking its prey. I stared with wide eyes in amazement while my cousin turned to me and whispered, "Let's go home and get a gun."

The excitement of discovery turned into the emotional rush of the hunt. We ran the half mile back to my house, sneaked past our mothers, and ran back to the ditch. He carried my older brother's pellet gun, and I had the pellets jammed into my pants pockets.

The egret had disappeared so we began searching along the grassy bank. On one side of us, the first green shoots of a vineyard reached upward, stretching for the sun. On the other side lay a ditch thirty feet across, a seasonal river carrying water to thirsty fields. As we marched, the water silently drifted in the opposite direction. Occasionally a peach branch or a gnarled old vine stump floated in the current, along with some trash which seemed to multiply each year.

We talked, the thrill of the hunt alive in our veins. Images swept through my mind—the rush of wings, the great white bird heaving itself into the air, the crack of the gun. I imagined witnessing the creature suspended in the air, shot and conquered. We'd both meet for that moment, a shot penetrating the white feathers, piercing deep into the flesh. Then the body would buckle, collapse, and fall into the water. The splash of the hunted, my prey conquered, cleansed, and cooled by water.

My cousin grabbed my arm, squeezing hard. It hurt. I spun and tried to jerk free. "There she is," he said.

I looked up. Across the ditch the egret stood motionless, her white body frozen against the gentle swaying of the ditch bank grasses. She was hidden from the road and protected by the farmlands around her. But we stood thirty-five feet away on the opposite side, separated by the river of water.

"We gotta go back, cross the bridge to get a better shot," my cousin whispered. We tried to walk slowly, but anxious feet shuffled and then scurried down the dirt trail. We pretended we were Indians, walking without breaking a stick, silent stalkers of nature. We ended up running down the road, back over the bridge, dashing toward our prey.

I had expected the egret to be scared and take flight. I imagined her rise, each flap of wings propelling her higher and higher away from us, saving herself and us.

My cousin's arm thumped against my chest, almost knocking me over. "Give me a bullet," he ordered.

With sweaty hands I fumbled in my tight pants for a pellet. Bullet? I said to myself. I had never called them bullets.

He loaded, crouched low, and walked up the bank. I watched as he peered over the edge and raised the gun. Then he pushed the muzzle into the weeds, maneuvering closer to the creature. At point-blank range, he squeezed a shot.

I ran and watched the great white bird slump into the water. There was no flight, no spreading of wings, and no soaring. The egret rolled into the water with hardly a splash.

My cousin held out his hand for one more pellet but I wouldn't give him another. I distracted him by pointing out that our prey was now drifting downstream with the current. He turned and we both watched it float away. Then I broke and ran along the ditch bank. My cousin stood angrily, cursing the water.

I caught up to the great white carcass as it rode the silent stream, and then ran as fast as I could to the bridge to beat the current. I stood over the water, waiting for the white mass of feathers. It slowly drifted toward me and slipped under the bridge. I ran to the other side and for a moment it failed to appear, as if it all had been a dream. But then the body slipped out from the darkness and into the brilliant sunlight. I watched it float downstream until it became a white blur.

EVERY WINTER WHEN I walk my fields, I see a white egret on the ditch bank. I stop my work and watch her, keeping my distance and staying in my vineyard.

The creature stands motionless. Each of us studies the other. Then the egret crouches, bends her legs, and launches herself upward toward the heavens. I watch her spread her wings wide and, with each stroke, soar higher aloft, circling the farm and me.

I hope she will see the green of my winter cover crops and lush fields, that she can imagine the brilliant colors of spring wildflowers and crimson clovers. I hope she feels the abundant life in my orchards and vineyards, from the soil full of earthworms to the diverse clovers, vetches, and weeds. I hope she realizes I now grow grapes and peaches and a habitat for a universe of insects and small creatures.

I watch the egret circle above me, hoping she'll once again come back to my fields.

# acknowledgments

Just as I cannot farm alone, I cannot write alone. Many thanks to my family for their help and wisdom, from long conversations with my dad to Marcy patiently listening and supporting my writing. I thank my relatives, neighbors, and cherished friends who encourage my work. I am also fortunate to have farmer friends who continue to inspire me with their daily work and artistry.

A special thanks to Elizabeth Wales, who believes in my voice, and Caroline Pincus, for her hours of editing and caring.

And I am grateful to all who still appreciate the wonderful taste of a good peach.